Laying the Foundation

A Family Study of the Apostle's Creed

By Luke Gilkerson

Laying the Foundation: A Family Study of the Apostle's Creed

By: Luke Gilkerson
Cover Design: Sarah Thomas

Intoxicated on Life • Copyright 2014 Luke Gilkerson

THE APOSTLES' CREED

I believe in God, the Father Almighty,
the Maker of heaven and Earth,
and in Jesus Christ, His only Son, our Lord:
Who was conceived by the Holy Ghost,
born of the virgin Mary,
suffered under Pontius Pilate, was crucified, dead, and buried;
He descended into hell.
The third day He arose again from the dead;
He ascended into heaven,
and sitteth on the right hand of God the Father Almighty;
from thence he shall come to judge the quick and the dead.
I believe in the Holy Ghost;
the holy catholic church; the communion of saints;
the forgiveness of sins;
the resurrection of the body;
and the life everlasting.
Amen.

TABLE OF CONTENTS

INTRODUCTION FOR PARENTS

The Apostles' Creed is one of the oldest Christian creeds, confessed by believers for more than 1,600 years—and older versions date back to some of the earliest days of the church.

It is common today, especially among Evangelicals, to fear formal creeds as somehow *replacing* the Bible, but this was not a fear shared by the original Reformers. The Creed *assumes* the authority of the Bible by borrowing the very language of Scripture for its content.

Confession of the Apostles' Creed in the Roman Catholic Church is still common today, but it is also common in many Protestant churches. When Reformer Martin Luther was compiling his Small Catechism for Christian families, he included what he considered three essentials: the Ten Commandments, the Lord's Prayer, and the Apostles' Creed. The Anglican *Book of Common Prayer* and the Heidelberg Catechism contain the same three essentials. Both Calvin and Zwingli included it among their doctrinal norms. It is also cited in full at the end of the oldest editions of the 1647 Westminster Shorter Catechism.

Luther said of the Apostles' Creed, "Christian truth could not possibly be put into a shorter and clearer statement." John Calvin set the Creed to music so it could be used for public worship. John Wesley called the Apostles' Creed a "beautiful summary" of the essential truths of our faith, and when writing the evening prayer service for Methodists, he included the recitation of the Creed.

The Apostles' Creed has an honored place in many Christian traditions, but what value does it have for Christian families today?

1. The Creed gives our children essentials of the faith.

Creeds remind us that there are some beliefs worth *fighting* for. We should strive to rightly interpret and believe *all* God has revealed, but creeds help us to remember there are some matters of "first importance" (1 Corinthians 15:3).

Most creeds are formed in times of heresy. As heretical sects arose in the church, the church fathers would point to the traditions passed down to them by the Apostles—and of course the writings of the Apostles—to crush heresies that were threatening the gospel.

Orthodox creeds like the Apostles' Creed give our children accurate summaries of the essentials. And as heresies arise today, our children will be more equipped to say, "This is not what I was taught. This is not the faith handed down to us from Christ."

This is why we should teach kids the Apostles' Creed: it states in simple, Scriptural language the essential facts of our faith as God has revealed them, from the creation of the world to Christ's redeeming work to eternal life in the world to come.

2. The Creed teaches our kids that Christianity is "confessional."

For the last couple hundred years, Western Christianity, by and large, has moved away from the importance of creeds. In the interest of unity, some in the Church want to be minimalists when it comes to doctrine. "No creed but Christ, no book but the Bible," they say. As well intentioned as this is, it overlooks two facts: (1) "no creed but Christ" is functionally a type of creed anyway, and (2) the apostles themselves stressed the importance of creeds.

The Apostles did not just write sacred Scripture; they also summarized essentials of the gospel in creedal statements. The first creed of the New Testament is "Jesus is Lord" (Romans 10:9; cf. 1 Corinthians 12:3; 2 Corinthians 4:5; Philippians 2:11). The Christian was one who "received Christ Jesus the Lord" (Colossians 2:6), confessing that Jesus is God's Son, come in the flesh (1 John 2:23; 4:2-3; 4:15; 2 John 7). These short statements summarize the believer's loyalty and commitment to Jesus Christ, and they state truths about Jesus in his relation to God.

Other examples of apostolic creeds include 1 Corinthians 15:3-8, Ephesians 4:4-6, 1 Timothy 3:16, and Philippians 2:6-11. The Apostles taught the church to be confessional: to provide believers with formal, verbal summaries of the faith.

3. The Creed teaches our children to value tradition.

Many in today's culture devalue the past. But as Christians, we should celebrate tradition.

It is important not to confuse *tradition* with *traditionalism*. Jaroslav Pelikan wisely stated, "Tradition is the living faith of the dead; traditionalism is the dead faith of the living." As Christians we should take joy in the living faith of those who came before us, those whose lives were radically changed by the gospel, who fought to pass the gospel on to the next generation.

Far from being a cold, lifeless, abstract text, church historian Philip Schaff says the Apostles' Creed is "a profession of living facts and saving truths. It is a liturgical poem and an act of worship."

4. The Creed teaches our children that Christianity is personal but not private.

When families and churches recite the Apostles' Creed, they are reciting something deeply personal, starting with the phrase "I believe." The Creed was written as a personal statement of faith, and this is something all parents should stress to their kids. Merely reciting the words isn't nearly as important as really *believing* them.

But in our increasingly relativistic age, we fight a culture that believes that *personal* faith is meant to be kept *private*. "It's fine if you have your personal beliefs, as long as you don't try to pass them on to others." But creeds are written not merely as personal statements, but as public declarations said by whole communities. The very reason why creeds are formulated is to pass the essentials of the faith on to future generations.

5. The Creed connects our children to their Christian heritage.

Early church fathers, following in the footsteps of the Apostles, formulated what they called the "Rule of Faith" (*Regula Fidei*), meaning a "measure" or "ruler" or orthodoxy. In the second and third centuries, this Rule of Faith was also called "the tradition," "the preaching," and the "Rule of Truth." Church father Origen described it as "the teaching of the church preserved unaltered and handed down in unbroken succession from the apostles."

This "Rule" was passed on via oral tradition, and while it varied in form and content, its core was similar from church to church. In the late second century, Irenaeus was the first to record a version of the Rule of Faith in written form:

> "...this faith: in one God, the Father Almighty, who made the heaven and the earth and the seas and all that are in them; and in one Christ Jesus, the Son of God, who was made flesh for our salvation; and in the Holy Spirit, who made known through the prophets the plan of salvation, and the coming, and the birth from a virgin, and the passion, and the resurrection from the dead, and the bodily ascension into heaven of the beloved Christ Jesus , our Lord, and his future appearing from heaven in the glory of the Father to sum up all things and to raise up anew all flesh of the whole human race..."

Similar creedal statements are found in various forms and are discussed in the writings of others like Justin Martyr, Tertullian, and Origen.

A disciple of Irenaeus, Hippolytus, recorded what would become known as the "Old Roman Creed" in AD 215, which was used for baptism candidates in the church at Rome. Notice how similar it is to the present day Apostles' Creed:

> I believe in God the Father almighty
> and in Christ Jesus His only Son, our Lord
> Who was born from the Holy Spirit and the Virgin Mary
> Who was under Pontius Pilate, was crucified and buried,
> on the third day rose again from the dead,
> ascended into heaven,
> sits at the right hand of the Father,
> whence He will come to judge the living and the dead;
> and in the Holy Spirit,
> the holy Church
> the remission of sins,
> the resurrection of the flesh.

This practice to recite the Old Roman Creed before baptism spread to other churches and became a widespread practice.

This creed was first called the Apostles' Creed (*Symbolum Apostolorum*) in AD 390 in a letter addressed to Pope Siricius by the Council of Milan. Variations in this Creed were worked out by the seventh century.

As we teach our children the Apostles' Creed, we should help them to appreciate that they are reciting a confession of faith that has been uttered by countless millions of Christians throughout the ages.

A Note About the Origin of the Apostles' Creed

Does the Rule of Faith go back to the Apostles themselves? We don't know. But the oral tradition that contained these core truths is possibly as old AD 100. The Rule of Faith was a measure for the proper reading of the Scriptures.

It was believed throughout the Middle Ages that, on the day of Pentecost, the twelve Apostles were inspired by the Holy Spirit to pen the Apostles' Creed—each Apostle contributing one of twelve articles. This belief is foreshadowed in a sermon by Ambrose, the Bishop of Milan, in the late fourth century, who wrote that the Creed was "pieced together by twelve workmen." Soon after, Rufinus of Aquileia wrote something similar, stating the Creed was the joint work of all the Apostles on the day of Pentecost. By the sixth century, the complete legend had developed.

This story, as far as church historians can tell, is unhistorical. It is a legend that gave credence to the use of the Creed in the church.

A Note About "He Descended into Hell"

See the appendix for a more detailed description of this phrase.

This phrase is one of the more controversial phrases in the whole Creed. It is a late edition to the Creed, but the belief in Christ's descent was a very early belief in the church. Many today still believe in Christ's descent into the underworld after death. Others choose not to include it in the Creed or retranslate it to make the meaning clearer to modern hearers.

In this study, we have taken a cautious approach to the phrase. The earliest church traditions emphasized several things about Christ's descent, and we are emphasizing two themes in particular. (1) The phrase means that, as a man, Christ truly died. His soul was separated from His body, and He experienced a real death. (2) The phrase means Christ's soul departed to be in Paradise (Luke 23:43) to be with saints who had departed before Him.

Other questions about Christ's descent are left unaddressed in this study. Did Christ rescue the saints from some kind of captivity? Was Paradise located in the underworld (Hades) or in heaven? Did He preach to the saints and/or to fallen angels? These questions are explored more in the appendix.

A Note About the "Holy Catholic Church"

The term "catholic" is interpreted broadly as the universal, comprehensive church. The emphasis here is not Roman Catholic vs. Protestant or Eastern Orthodox, but the broad, worldwide church.

A Note About the "Communion of Saints"

This phrase was a late addition to the Creed and has been the subject of much discussion. The phrase started to appear in the late fourth century in various creeds and eventually found its way into the Apostles' Creed.

Generally speaking, all agree that the phrase refers to the togetherness of the church, the people of God as one body united in Christ. The original Latin phrase was understood as "communion of holy people" (saints) or "communion of holy things" (specifically, the elements of the Lord's Supper). In the early church, the first meaning became dominant, but it was generally understood that this phrase had strong sacramental implications: the fellowship and unity of God's people was expressed visibly by participation in the Eucharist. In this study, we focus on the first meaning.

The early church also believed that the communion of saints includes not only all the saints spread throughout the world, but all the departed saints as well. This truth is expressed in Hebrews 12:22-24, where the living readers are said to be in communion with God, the worshipping angels, and the spirits of the righteous made perfect. This is a profound and rich doctrine that is worth exploring, but in this study, the communion of the saints on Earth is the primary focus.

HOW TO USE THIS STUDY

This study is designed for you to spend 30 days in a row studying the Apostles' Creed with your children, working through one lesson each day. This will immerse your children in the text.

You could also spend 30 weeks doing one lesson each week. You might choose to do this over the duration of one school year.

I would suggest using not one, but both of these approaches, particularly if you will be memorizing this passage of Scripture. Spend 30 straight days going through this study to acquaint your family with the text prior to memorizing the text. This will help them understand why you are memorizing it. Then, repeat the Bible study weekly throughout the year to study this Scripture at a slower pace and reinforce the lessons that were already covered once. Repetition is the mother of learning.

Make it a Goal to Memorize

Over the next several months or throughout an entire school year, make a commitment to memorize all of the Apostles' Creed as a family.

There is great benefit to memorizing Scripture and ancient creeds and confessions, and an added benefit to memorizing a lengthier text like this. Memorizing a whole chapter of the Bible or longer text gives our children a sense of context.

Memory Method: Using Scripture Memory Cards

One of the best ways to move Scripture and other memorized texts from short-term to long-term memory is to use a Charlotte Mason-style "memory box."

Become a subscriber at intoxicatedonlife.com/freebies and you'll get access to free printables. There, the Apostles' Creed is divided into manageable sections (2-3 lines) on individual index cards.

You'll also find free printable tabbed dividers to help organize all your cards. You'll find...

- A tab marked "Daily"
- A tab marked "Odd Days" and another marked "Even Days"
- Weekly tabs (a tab for each day of the week)
- Monthly tabs (tabs numbered 1-30)

Here's how it works:

1. Place all your tabbed dividers into the box in order.
2. Start by placing the first Apostles' Creed card behind the "Daily" tab. Review this card with your child daily, having him or her recite it aloud.
3. Once your child can quote an entire card from memory with ease, move it back to either the "odd" tab or "even" tab. Then, only review that card on odd or even dates of the month.
4. Once your child continues to quote the card without help for a couple weeks, move it back to one of the weekly tabs.
5. If they can quote the card several weeks in a row without help, then move it back to one of the monthly tabs.
6. As cards move out from behind the daily tab, add new cards to the daily memory time.

Use Handwriting to Teach

In Deuteronomy 17:18-19, the kings of Israel were commanded to write out for themselves a copy of the law of Moses so that they could read it all the days of their lives. God clearly sees value in not only reading the Bible daily, but also in copying the text of the Bible by hand.

A good way to reinforce memory (and practice handwriting skills) is to copy texts by hand. **As a companion to this study, you can get a copy of our Apostles' Creed version of *Write Through the Bible*, available at intoxicatedonlife.com.**

These workbooks take 38 days to complete and combine the disciplines of handwriting, dictation, vocabulary, and memory into one daily activity. The *Write Through the Bible* downloadable workbooks are available in both manuscript and cursive and in either KJV or ESV translations.

LESSON 1: The Creed

Opening Thought:

If I had a really important announcement that I wanted you to remember, what could I do to help you not forget it? (*See what ideas your child comes up with.*)

I could do a lot of things. I could write down that really important thing and give the paper to you. Later, you could pull out that piece of paper and remember what I said. I could also tell you over and over and over to help you remember it. I could also tell other people the important announcement so a bunch of people could remember it, couldn't I?

About 2000 years ago, a group of men had a very important message. It was an amazing message about God and the great things they saw God do. But they didn't want people to forget it after they were gone. They knew one day they would be dead and they didn't want others to forget what they said.

Let's read part of one of the letters these men wrote.

Scripture Reading: 2 Thessalonians 2:13-15

Explanation: Paul, the man who wrote this letter, was writing to Christians whom he knew and loved. He reminds them the first time he met these people he told them a wonderful message called "the gospel." The word "gospel" means "good news." This was good news about someone the readers had never heard about before: Jesus. Can you think of any stories you know about Jesus? (*See what kind of stories your kids can remember.*)

Paul says his readers should hold on to the teachings and traditions he taught them. After they started believing in Jesus, Paul taught them great truths about God and he didn't want them to forget. Paul says he taught them in two ways: by speaking to them personally and by writing letters to them.

Men like Paul were called "apostles." This means they were people who Jesus personally sent out to lead the church and teach others about Him. These apostles wrote a lot of information down about Jesus so we wouldn't forget. In fact, everything in the New Testament was written by an apostle or someone who studied closely with an apostle.

(Pick up your Bible and show your child the New Testament. Flip through some of the books and see if you or your child can figure out who the author is on specific books.)

All of these apostles eventually died: Paul, Peter, John, Matthew, and others left us their writings. But they didn't just write things down. They also trained *new* leaders in the church to teach after they were gone. Those leaders trained more leaders who also taught more people about Jesus. Those church leaders didn't want people to forget the important things the apostles taught, so they made lists of the most important things we should remember about Jesus.

These lists are sometimes called "creeds." The word "creed" comes from an old Latin word "credo," which means, "I believe." These were lists of things that Christians believed. These were the *most important* things Christians needed to remember about the gospel, the good news.

We're going to be studying something called the "Apostles' Creed." It wasn't written by the apostles. It was written by church leaders who came *after* the apostles' who said, "These are the things the apostles taught that were most important. These are the things they didn't want us to forget. These are the things every Christian should believe." Did you know that today people all over the world *still* say the Apostles' Creed out loud in churches as a way to worship God?

The Apostles' Creed tells us a great story about the things God has done, starting all the way back when He created the world, to the time when Jesus came, to the time when Jesus will come back again in the future and make everything right.

Questions for Your Kids:

1. So, let's see if you remember: what's the name given to the special people that Jesus sent to lead the church and tell others about Him? (*Apostles*)

2. And what were the main ways the apostles taught the church about Jesus? (*They wrote things down and they taught people personally.*)

3. What is the creed we're studying called? (*The Apostles' Creed*)

4. What is a creed? (*Your child may remember that "creed" comes from the Latin word that means, "I believe." A creed is a brief statement about what Christians believe.*)

Prayer: *For your prayer, read aloud the Apostles' Creed in full. You may want to add your own personal prayer at the end.*

I believe in God, the Father Almighty,
  the Maker of heaven and Earth,
and in Jesus Christ, His only Son, our Lord:
  Who was conceived by the Holy Ghost,
    born of the virgin Mary,
  suffered under Pontius Pilate, was crucified, dead, and buried;
    He descended into hell.
  The third day He arose again from the dead;
  He ascended into heaven,
    and sitteth on the right hand of God the Father Almighty;
  from thence he shall come to judge the quick and the dead.
I believe in the Holy Ghost;
  the holy catholic church; the communion of saints;
  the forgiveness of sins;
  the resurrection of the body;
  and the life everlasting.
Amen.

LESSON 2: I Believe

Opening Thought:

Let me start with a story. Two men stood at the end of a huge cliff with a big pit at the bottom. In front of them was a bridge going over the large pit to the other side and was attached to another cliff. Both men looked the bridge and were scared to walk on it because the cliff was so high. Both of them asked each other, "Do you believe the bridge is strong enough to hold us?" Both of them said, "Yes, I believe that." But the first man didn't get on the bridge. Only the second man actually stepped on the bridge and walked to the other side.

Did both men really believe the bridge was strong enough, or just the one who walked across? (*See what your kids say. Ask them, "If the first man really believed it was strong enough, why didn't he walk across it?" What does it really mean to "believe" something?*)

Scripture Reading: James 2:14-19

Explanation: The word "faith" is another way to talk about belief. If you have faith in something, it means you believe in it. The author of this passage says there's a big difference between *dead* faith and *living* faith.

You have dead faith if you just say you believe but it doesn't change the way you live. The author gives two examples of this. The first example is of a person who says he's a believer in Christ, says he is a Christian, but when he sees another Christian friend in great need, he doesn't do anything to help. He doesn't feel any pity or love. He sees the man with no clothes and no food and does nothing. This kind of person has dead faith. Why do you think it's called "dead" faith? (*See what your child says. Faith is dead because it's like a dead plant: it doesn't produce any leaves or fruit, it doesn't make someone live differently.*)

The second example given is demons. Demons are evil angels, terrible spirits who don't obey God. Even demons believe that God is real and that He is the only God, but this doesn't mean they love God. They are afraid of God, but they don't try to obey Him. Even demons have dead faith.

If they had living faith, things would be different. If your faith is alive, it changes the way you act. It's like the man who walked across the bridge: he had *living* faith in the bridge. He really *trusted* that the bridge wouldn't fall. He showed his faith by his actions.

The beginning of the Apostles' Creed says, "I believe." This is not talking about just any kind of belief. It is talking about *living faith*. When we say we believe in God, or we believe in Jesus, we are really saying, "I trust God." We're saying, "My trust in God makes me want to follow Him, makes me want to obey Him."

Questions for Your Kids:

1. If someone asked you if you believe that God exists, what would you say? (*See what your child says. Remember to probe deeper. Does your child say he or she believes in God? Ask what your child believes about God.*)

2. If someone asked you if you believe in Jesus, what would you say? (*See what your child says. Remember to probe deeper. Does your child say he or she believes in Jesus? Ask why. Ask what your child believes about Jesus. If he or she doesn't know, tell them that this is what this study of the Apostles' Creed is all about: to learn the truth about Jesus.*)

3. If a person with dead faith says, "I believe in God," does that person want to follow God or obey Him? (*No. He might follow God sometimes when he feels like it, but he doesn't really put all of his confidence in God. Deep down he wants other things more than he wants God.*)

Prayer: "Search us, God, and know our hearts. See if there is anything sinful in us (Psalm 139:23-24). Help us to test ourselves, to see whether we really have living faith (2 Corinthians 13:5). We want to add to our faith goodness, self-control, and godliness so we can be sure that we really belong to You (2 Peter 1:5-11). Amen."

LESSON 3: I Believe in God

Opening Thought:

Let's say someone came up to you and said, "You believe in God? That's silly. You can't even see God! Why would you believe in something you can't see?" What would you say to that person? (*See what answers your child comes up with. Perhaps your child won't know what to say. That's okay. Ask your child to think about other things they can't see that they know exist: air, thoughts in other people's minds, etc.*)

The very first phrase of the Apostles' Creed is "I believe in God." We're going to talk about who God is and why we believe He exists.

Scripture Reading: Romans 1:18-23

Explanation: This passage is interesting because it is talking about people who don't act like they believe in God. They don't thank God for the good things He's given us. They don't worship God as their Creator. They don't try to make God the most important thing in their lives. Instead, they find other things to worship. They make their lives all about other things and ignore God.

Over the centuries, people have come up with all kinds of reasons why people should believe in God. Some say, "Look at how organized the world is, how beautiful nature is! The only way our world could be so ordered and so beautiful is if a wise Creator designed it." Have you ever looked out into nature, maybe looked up at the stars in the sky, and thought that? (*See what your child says about this. Tell them about something in the natural world you have seen that made you stop and think about God.*)

Others say, "How did the world get here at all? Something had to cause the world to exist. Something had to start it all, and it had to be Someone who is powerful enough to create everything."

This Bible passage says, deep down, everyone *already believes* in God. God has made it obvious to everyone: when we look out into the created world, we can all see that there must be a God who has great power and is eternal—a God who has always existed. But this passage says when people want to continue sinning, following their own way, they find that part of their heart that believes in God and they silence it. They try to ignore it. Why do you think people try to forget that God exists? (*See what your child says.*)

A lot of the world doesn't like Christianity because it reminds them that there is a God who created everything and who is worthy to be worshipped. People don't want to believe that, because if that is true, it means they have to stop living in a sinful way. All of us are like that. If God let us, we would all walk away from God and ignore Him, but there would always be this part of us, deep down, that thought about God.

When we say the Apostles' Creed, and when we start by saying, "I believe in God," we're really saying, "I have always believed in God, because I can look out into the world God made and see that He must be real. But I'm not trying to silence that belief anymore. I'm not ignoring God. I don't just believe He's real; I am also trying to make God the most important person in my life."

Questions for Your Kids:

1. Deep down, does everyone believe in God? (*Yes, on some level they do.*)

2. Why do people act like God isn't real? Why do they ignore God if they believe He is real? (*Because they want to go on sinning and living their own lives.*)

3. We believe in God and we try to remember Him in our daily lives. Does that make us better or smarter than those people who are trying to ignore God? (*No. If God left us, we would all ignore Him.*)

4. If someone came up to us and said, "I don't believe in God," what might we say to them? (*Think along with your child about ways you could respond. Think about the evidence for God's existence seen in creation. Think about the history of God's people, and especially the miraculous things Jesus did, that remind you that God is real.*)

Prayer: "God, the fool says in his heart, 'There is no god.' We don't want to be foolish and ignore you (Psalm 14:1; 53:1). But even the fish in the sea and the birds in the sky know You are real (Job 12:7-10). We believe that You exist and that You reward those who earnestly seek You (Hebrews 11:6). When we look into creation, when we lift up our eyes and see the stars You've created, we know that no one compares to You, God (Isaiah 40:25-26). Help us to always remember how real You are. Amen."

LESSON 4: Father, Son, & Spirit

Opening Thought:

(*Get out a piece of paper and draw a few stick-figure people on the page.*) We'll call this piece of paper Flat Land. Let's say these people here lived in Flat Land. They lived on this flat piece of paper their whole lives. If they wanted to look around, they could only look along the plane of the paper. If they wanted to move, they could only move side to side, back and forth. (*Draw lines from the people in different directions on the page.*) They can't move or see up and down. (*Move the pen or pencil from the paper up into the air as if drawing an imaginary line above the page.*)

Let's say one day I use some magic, and I become a stick person and enter Flat Land. (*Draw a new stick figure that looks like you.*) Let's say I walk around on their piece of paper and I talk to them and make friends with them. If I tried explaining what up and down was (*draw your imaginary lines up in the air again*), they would probably scratch their heads and be confused. They've never seen up and down. They've never moved up and down. They only know side to side, back and forth. If I try to tell them that there are people who live in a world where you can move not just back and forth, side to side, but also up and down, their minds couldn't understand what up and down means. When they see the world, they can only look along the plane of the paper.

Think about that as we read our text today, because I'm about to tell you something about God that will be hard to understand, just like Flat Land people would have a hard time understanding us.

Scripture Reading: Mark 1:1-11

Explanation: This is the story of Jesus' baptism by John the Baptist in the Jordan River. The text says when Jesus came up out of the water, something amazing happened. He looked up, and he saw the sky open up and the Spirit of God came down on Jesus like a dove. He also heard a voice telling Him, "You are my beloved Son. I am well pleased with you."

We see three main characters in this story: God the Father who speaks from heaven, God the Son, Jesus, who is baptized, and God the Holy Spirit who comes down on Jesus. Here's the strange thing: *all three* of them are called God in the Bible, and the Bible also says there is only *one* God. Does this sound confusing to you? Have you heard of this before? (*See how your child reacts to this.*)

When people wrote down the Apostles' Creed they made three main sections for it: the beginning speaks of God the Father creating the world, the middle part speaks about God the Son, Jesus Christ, coming to save us, and the end part begins with God the Holy Spirit. They wrote it this way because the Bible tells us that God is not *one person* but *three persons*.

Later on, the church called this the Trinity. God is one God, but He is three persons. All three have been around for eternity. All three are equal in power and glory. This can be hard to understand for us.

Don't think of the Trinity as three gods: God the Father, Son, and Holy Spirit are one spiritual being. You can't divide them from each other. They always act together. We also shouldn't think of the Trinity as one person playing three different parts, like an actor who wears three different masks in a play. The story of Jesus' baptism shows this: they are three different persons.

How can this be? It doesn't make sense to us because down here on Earth, I am only one person. You are only one person. Everyone we know is only one person. We don't know someone who is three persons at the same time.

We're like people living in Flat Land who can't picture what up and down is. Flat Land people can only understand back and forth, side to side. Their minds can't even grasp the idea of depth or moving up and down.

God is *one* God, but *three* persons. He has always been that way: each person of the Trinity loves the others with a perfect love, and they are always in perfect harmony with each other. It is a big mystery, but all three of these persons are involved in our salvation, and as we study the Apostles' Creed more, you'll see how.

Questions for Your Kids:

1. So, let's see if you get what I'm talking about. Is God really three gods? (*No. That's not correct. For older kids you can mention that this false idea is called "tritheism": the belief in three gods. This is opposed to monotheism: the belief in one God.*)

2. Is God one person just playing three different parts at different times? (*No. That's not correct. For older kids you can mention that this false idea is called "modalism": the one God has three different modes or three different ways He appears to us.)*

3. Is there any person in the Trinity who is more worthy of our worship than the others? (*No. All three are God. All three should be worshipped.)*

4. Did one of the persons in the Trinity come first? Did one of them exist before the other ones existed? (*No. All three have been around forever.)*

Prayer: "God, You are the first and the last. Besides You, there is no god (Isaiah 44:6). We try to understand You, God, but Your greatness is unsearchable (Psalm 145:3). When we think about You, God, all we can say is that this knowledge is too wonderful for us; we cannot fit You into our minds (Psalm 139:6). Your ways are beyond anything we can imagine (Romans 11:33). We want to get to know each Person of the Trinity, so we pray that the grace of the Lord Jesus Christ and the love of God the Father and the fellowship of the Holy Spirit is with us as we study these things (2 Corinthians 13:14). Amen."

LESSON 5: Maker

Opening Thought:

What is your favorite animal? (*Have your child share what his or her favorite animal is. Ask why it is a favorite.*)

Who made that animal? (*God*)

Think about all the other animals God made. Do you know how many different kinds of animals there are? (*See if your child can guess.*) Scientists have found more than 8 million different types of animals. Think also about the stars in the sky. Do you know how many stars there are? Using just our eyes, if we could travel the world and look at all the stars above us, we would count about 9,000 stars, but the galaxy we live in has more than 400 billion stars. We can't even imagine a number that large.

God is the One who made it all. The Apostles' Creed says God is the "Maker of heaven and Earth." Let's read a song in the Bible that celebrates God as the creator.

Scripture Reading: Psalm 104:1-5, 10-15, 19-24

Explanation: This psalm talks about the God as the king of the universe. Back when this was written, when a king had great power, he would wear big, expensive robes, he would live in a huge palace, and he would ride in a powerful chariot. The poet here is saying God is the greatest king. All the light in the universe is His robe because He is so glorious. The heavens above, filled with millions of stars, are His palace. His chariot is made of clouds, driven by horses of wind.

Let me ask you, do you think the poet's point is that God literally rides on clouds or that God wears a robe of light? (*No.*) The point is that if you think earthly kings are rich and powerful, God is richer and more powerful than you could ever imagine. The whole universe is His and all of nature is at His command.

The psalm also talks about how God is a master architect: He designed and built everything that exists. God created the earth, the deep valleys, tall mountains, rivers and streams, all the creatures on land, all the creatures that fly, and the plants people use to make food. God made the sun and the moon to give us times of day and night. God even created things we don't typically see, like the angels who serve as His messengers. When we see the created world, we are meant to praise God because He is powerful enough to make it all and wise enough to know how to make it all.

But this psalm tells us something else about our Creator. He didn't just create the world and step away from it. Some people believe that God just made us and then leaves us alone, but that isn't true. He is involved in the created world even right now. God controls when the winds blow and when the rain comes. He controls the water in the streams. He is the one who causes plants to grow. When the animals are waiting to find food, or when people are waiting for crops to grow, God is the one they are waiting for.

This is so important because this means everything that happens in creation is not a surprise to God. He's the one who controls when we have a lot and when we have only a little. He is in control of every situation. This means when things aren't going well for us, we can be patient, knowing that God is in control. When things are going well, we can be thankful, knowing God is the One who is making it happen. No matter what happens, we can trust God as the king of the universe.

Questions for Your Kids:

1. Is there anywhere in creation or is there anything you've seen in creation that has made you feel like, "Wow, God You are amazing"? Can you think of any time you felt that way? (*See what your child says. If they can't think of anything, tell them your own story about when that has happened to you.*)

2. Who created you? (*God.*)

3. When bad things happen in the world, is God still in control of those things? (*Yes. Nothing is a surprise to God. Nothing is outside of His control.*)

4. If bad things happen to us, should we worry and complain to God? How should we act? (*No. We should trust God instead. If God is wise enough to know how to make millions of animals and billions of stars, then He is wise enough to know how to control everything according to His big plan. We may not know His plan, but we can trust that He is wise. We can also pray to Him knowing He has the power to change things.*)

Prayer: "God, You are worthy to receive glory and honor, because You created all things, and by Your will they exist (Revelation 4:11). You sustain everything You created by your powerful word (Hebrews 1:3). All over the world, You give rains and fruitful seasons. You satisfy people with food and gladness (Acts 14:15). We can never say that You are out of control or that You don't know about our situation. You are the everlasting God who created the stars in the sky and the earth beneath us. Your wisdom is bigger than anything we can imagine. You never run out of energy or get tired (Isaiah 40:21-31). Help us to trust You in all situations and help us to be thankful. Amen."

LESSON 6: God Almighty

Opening Thought:

How strong do you think you are? What's the heaviest think you can lift in this room? (*Listen to your child's answer. If they say something too small, encourage them to think bigger. Tell your child to try and lift it right now.*)

Is there something around here you know you can't lift up? (*See what your child says.*)

Can God lift that? (*Yes.*)

The Bible says that God is all-powerful. In fact, God calls Himself the "Almighty" God. When we read this story, be listening for the word "Almighty."

Scripture Reading: Genesis 17:1-8

Explanation: The story of Abraham in the Bible is very important. God made a special promise to Abraham called a "covenant." A covenant is like a special agreement where people make promises to be faithful to each other.

God makes some amazing promises to Abraham in this covenant. He promises that Abraham is going to be the father of many people, which is strange because in this story Abraham is 99 years old, and he and his wife are far too old to have children. He promises Abraham that He will give Abraham's children the land that he was traveling in, the land of Canaan.

God fulfilled these promises. First, even though Abraham and his wife Sarah were too old to have kids anymore, Sarah miraculously became pregnant, and that child grew up and had more children, and those children grew up and had more children. Over 400 years later, long after Abraham died, his family had grown into a huge nation, just like God said would happen.

Then, when the time was right, God brought that big nation into the land of Canaan so they could live there, just as God had promised. Have you heard some of these stories about how God brought them out of slavery and helped them to conquer their new land? (*See if your child has heard any of the stories, and which stories he or she remembers.*)

God performed many miracles for them. He sent deadly plagues against their enemies. He divided the deep waters of the sea so they could walk on the sea floor to get to the other side. He dried up rivers so they could cross. He made huge city walls fall down. He even made the sun stand still in the sky so they could win a battle.

God made promises to Abraham and He kept those promises. He could do this because He is God Almighty. This is how God introduces Himself to Abraham in this passage: He calls Himself the Almighty God.

The Apostles' Creed says, "I believe in God the Father Almighty." When we say we believe that God is Almighty, we mean He can do all things. He has made the world. He can control nature. He can destroy nations. He can divide a deep ocean or make the sun stand still in the sky. Nothing is impossible with God Almighty. He is able to do everything He promises.

Questions for Your Kids:

1. Can you remember the opening line of the Apostles' Creed? (*See if your child can recite it. It is, "I believe in God the Father Almighty, Maker of heaven and Earth."*)

2. What does almighty mean? (*God has the power to do anything He wants.*)

3. What are some of the great miracles God has done in the past? (*See how many different powerful miracles you child can name.*)

4. When God makes a promise in the Bible, is He always able to fulfill that promise? (*Yes. Every promise He makes He has the power to fulfill.*)

5. When God makes a special promise to someone, what is that promise called? (*A covenant*)

Prayer: "God, You are the Lord, the God of all flesh, and nothing is too hard for You; nothing is impossible for You (Jeremiah 32:27; Luke 1:37). When You have a plan, no one can ruin that plan (Job 42:2). Even when the world does evil things, even when we do evil things, You have the power to take those things and make them work for good (Romans 8:28). As we read the Bible and learn about Your covenant promises, help us to remember that You are God Almighty, and You can fulfill all Your promises. Amen."

LESSON 7: God the Father

Opening Thought:

Let's say there was a rich and powerful king. He had absolute power in his kingdom. He was always dressed in the finest robes and wearing his golden crown. When his subjects approached him, they stood at a distance because they were so fearful of his power. Picture yourself in that king's great hall. See the beautiful room, his golden throne, and all his subjects bowing down in front of him.

Now picture a little girl. She's the king's daughter. She runs through the great hall and yells, "Papa!" as she runs up to his throne and crawls up in his lap.

Can you imagine just *any* of that king's subjects doing that? (*No.*) The great king is not their father. To them, he is just a great and powerful ruler, someone to revere, someone even to fear. But, even though the little girl knows her dad is the king, he is her father first. She acts differently around him than others in the kingdom do.

That's the way it is with God. We've already talked about how God is the maker of heaven and Earth and how He is the "Almighty" God. There are many people in the world who believe these things about God, but the Apostles' Creed also says, "I believe in God *the Father*." To Christians, God isn't just a great and powerful Creator, He isn't just an Almighty God—He is also our Father.

Let's read what Jesus said about God the Father.

Scripture Reading: Matthew 6:25-34

Explanation: Three times in this passage Jesus says, "Do not be anxious." This means, "Don't worry." The people Jesus was talking to had a lot of worries. They worried about things like food, water, and clothing. There weren't big malls or stores you could go and buy whatever you needed. Most people had to grow or catch their own food. They had to make their own clothes. Many of them were very poor, so they worried about if they would have enough to eat or something warm to wear.

Jesus tells these disciples of His, "Being anxious, getting worried, is something only the Gentiles do." Who are the Gentiles? (*See if your child is familiar with that word.*) Gentile is a word that means "nation"—all the groups of people throughout the world who aren't part of God's special people. He says, "They worry about these things because they don't believe that God is their Father, but you do, so you don't need to worry." Gentiles worry about food and water and clothing because they believe it is all up to them. They don't realize that God is the one who provides for all their needs.

Picture a big flock of birds flying over their heads as Jesus says, "Look at the birds." Do birds build big barns to store their food? Do birds plant crops so they can have food? (*No.*) Jesus says, "Your heavenly Father feeds them." Perhaps there were a bunch of wildflowers around them, and Jesus told them to look at the flowers at their feet. Do flowers spend time making clothes? (*No.*) God makes flowers more beautiful than the richest king.

Let me ask you: Does God think you are more valuable than a bird? (*Yes.*) Are you more valuable to God than flowers? (*Yes.*) Does God take the time to feed the birds and make the flowers beautiful? (*Yes.*) So that means He's going to make sure your needs are met. God is a Father: He knows you better than you know yourself, He knows exactly what you need, and He loves you the way a good father loves his kids.

Questions for Your Kids:

1. Have you ever worried about something? What was it? (*Help your child to remember something he or she worried about.*)

2. How does worrying show a lack of faith? (*Faith is about trusting God and believing His promises. If we are worrying about something, it shows there's part of us that doesn't trust that God is going to take care of us.*)

3. Does God have the power to give you everything you need? (*Yes. He is God Almighty.*)

4. Does God have the desire to give you everything you need? (*Yes. He is God the Father.*)

Prayer: "Thank you, Father, that to all who receive Christ, to all who believe in His name, You have given them the right to become children of God (John 1:12). You have given us Your Holy Spirit that helps us to cry out 'Father' when we pray to You (Romans 8:15; Galatians 4:6). O God, the eyes of creatures look to You, and You give them their food when it is time (Psalm 145:15). Help us not to be anxious about anything we need in life, knowing that You are our Father, and You know exactly what we need. Amen."

LESSON 8:
Jesus

Opening Thought:

Did you know that people's names have meanings? It's true. Our names all come from different places in the world, and each name means something different.

(Look up the meanings of the names of your family members and share them. If you can't do that, use these names as examples.

- *"Samuel" means "his name is God."*
- *"Jacob" means "heel grabber"*
- *"Abigail" means "my father is joy"*
- *"Elizabeth" means "my God is an oath")*

Do you know that Jesus' name means something, too? That's what we're going to read about today.

Scripture Reading: Matthew 1:18-25

Explanation: Joseph was probably shocked to find out that the woman he was planning to marry was pregnant. He knew the child in Mary's womb wasn't his baby, so he planned on divorcing her.

One night, however, an angel came to Joseph in a dream to explain where this mysterious baby came from. This baby wasn't just any child. The Holy Spirit had come to Mary and performed a miracle, giving her a baby in her womb. The angel told Joseph to not be afraid to marry her.

Then the angel told Joseph what to name the child in her womb. The child's name should be "Jesus." In the Apostles' Creed, we say that we believe in "Jesus Christ." Let's look at this name "Jesus" a little closer.

It's interesting because Jesus was a fairly popular name back then. There were a lot of people named Jesus. Isn't it interesting that when the Son of God was born on Earth, God didn't give him a unique name—a name no one ever had? He gave Him a normal name. This is because Jesus is not just the Son of God. He is a human being.

But Jesus' name also means something special. His name is a combination of God's personal name from the Old Testament—Yahweh—and the word "salvation." Jesus' name means "God is salvation." The angel makes this very clear to Joseph: the baby should be called Jesus because He will *save* His people from their sins.

What is sin? (*See how your child answers this. Sin is disobeying or not following God's law in any way. Sin is a powerful drive in us that wants to forget about God and forget about helping others.*) When the angel tells Joseph that His name should "Jesus" because he will save us from our sins, this means two very important things. First, it means that Jesus saves us from the *guilt* of sin. When we sin, we should feel guilty because we are doing something bad and offending God. But Jesus came so we could be forgiven for all our sins.

Second, it means that Jesus saves us from the *grip* of sin. Sin is powerful because it is like a force in us that makes us want to do our own thing and just forget about God. But Jesus came to change us on the inside and make us want to follow God.

Jesus saves us from the *guilt* of our sin and the *grip* of sin.

Questions for Your Kids:

1. So, do you remember? What does Jesus' name mean? (*Yahweh is salvation or God is salvation*)

2. What does Jesus save us from? (*Sin*)

3. Can we save ourselves from our sin? (*No*)

4. Can anyone else save us from our sin? (*No*)

5. What does it mean that Jesus saves us from sin? (*Jesus rescues us from the guilt of sin and the grip of sin. He forgives us of our sins and He makes us want to stop sinning and follow God.*)

Prayer: "Thank you, God, for sending Jesus to us. He will save us completely from our sin (Hebrews 7:24-25). Jesus is the only name under heaven by which we must be saved (Acts 4:12). We know that at the name of Jesus someday every knee will bow in heaven and on Earth and under the earth, and every tongue will confess that Jesus Christ is Lord (Philippians 2:11). Teach us to love the name Jesus because we know it means He is our Savior. Amen."

LESSON 9: Christ

Opening Thought:

There are still some countries in the world that have kings and queens. Can you think of any? (*See if you child knows of any places in the world with reigning monarchs, places like the United Kingdom, Spain, Sweden, Norway, Japan, and others.*)

How do you become a king? Do you become a king if you get enough people to vote for you? (*No.*) When you are a king or queen, it's because you are born in the right family. You don't vote for kings. You are born into a royal family.

Today we'll read about the birth of the greatest king of all.

Scripture Reading: Luke 2:1-15

Explanation: This story is famous because it is usually read around Christmastime. It is the story of the birth of Jesus.

There are several important characters in this story. Can you think of the characters in this story? (*See how many characters your child can remember from the reading.*)

The most important character in the story is Jesus, of course.

Then there is Joseph and Mary. They arrive in Bethlehem because the government leaders want them to go there. Everyone who was going to Bethlehem then had one thing in common: they were all related to King David. David lived about a thousand years earlier and was one of the greatest kings the nation had ever seen. Bethlehem was where King David grew up. That's why this story calls Bethlehem the "city of David."

The most spectacular characters in the story are the angels. We don't know how many there were, but there must have been too many to count. At first only one appeared to announce that Jesus had been born, but then a multitude of them appeared, praising God.

The first angel tells the shepherds why the baby Jesus is so important. They tell them that the new baby is the "Christ." Do you know what the word "Christ" means? (*See if your child has heard the word before. He or she may have heard the name "Jesus Christ" before. The word "Christ" in Hebrew is "Messiah," and this means "Anointed.")*

Remember what I just said about King David—that great king from long ago? One day a famous prophet anointed David with oil, which was a special way kings were given power to lead their kingdom. God had made a special promise to King David. God promised him that his children and grandchildren and great-grandchildren and all his family would be the true rulers of Israel.

God's prophets also promised that there was one coming called *the* Anointed One, the ultimate King, the Messiah, the Christ. He would be born in David's family. He would be the true king of not just Israel but the whole world.

In the Apostles' Creed, when we say we believe in "Jesus Christ," we are saying we believe Jesus is the king God promised long ago. When the shepherds heard that the Christ, the Messiah, had been born, they were so amazed. Their people had been waiting for hundreds of years to get this news, and the true king, the Messiah, was finally here.

Questions for Your Kids:

1. Can you remember: what did the angels call Bethlehem? It was the city of __________. (*David.*) Why was it called that? (*It was where David grew up.*)

2. What does the word "Christ" mean? (*Messiah or Anointed. God promised to send the ultimate king, who would be part of David's family.*)

3. How was Jesus part of David's family? (*His earthly parents, Joseph and Mary, were descendants of King David.*)

4. One of the things good kings do is make laws and rule over their people. Does Jesus do that? (*Yes. Jesus rules over us through His Word, the Bible.*)

5. Another thing good kings do is they defend their people. How does Jesus do that for us? (*Jesus protects and guards us, keeping the forces of evil from capturing us, because we belong to God now. Nothing can tear us away from God because our King is powerful.*)

Prayer: "O Living God, we believe that your Son Jesus is the Christ (Matthew 16:16). He brought Your kingdom near to us (Matthew 4:17). You have given Him all authority in heaven and on Earth (Matthew 28:18). His kingdom will never end (Luke 1:33). You have given us eternal life, and no one can ever snatch us from our King's hand (John 10:28). We pray, give Christ the nations of the world. Give Him the ends of the earth as His possession, just as You said You would (Psalm 2:8). Amen."

LESSON 10: Our Lord

Opening Thought:

Do you know that a lot of the earliest Christians died because of what they believed? (*See if your child knows anything about that.*) There are still a lot of Christians who are hurt because of their faith, but in the first few hundred years of the church, the people who kill Christians most were their own government leaders.

Back then, most Christians lived in the Roman Empire, and the greatest person in that empire was their ruler. They called these people the Caesars. These men didn't just believe they were in charge, they also believed they were gods, that they should be worshiped. They built temples where people could worship them. They demanded that their subjects say, "Caesar is Lord!" Many Christians refused to do this because they knew Caesar wasn't a god, and they had only one they called "Lord." That Lord is Jesus.

Let's read a passage from the Bible about that.

Scripture Reading: Philippians 2:5-11

Explanation: This text is probably one of the earliest songs ever written about Jesus. It is a song about the great things Jesus did for us: how He let go of His position of glory and majesty and came to Earth as a man, how He lived as a man, how He suffered and died as a man, and how God raised Him up. Jesus obeyed His Father right up to the very end of His life.

Because He did this, God the Father gave to Jesus a name that is above every name. He gave Him the name "Lord." In earlier books of the Bible, the title "Lord" was for God alone. God said through the great prophet Isaiah, "I am the Lord, and there is no other, besides me there is no God" (Isaiah 45:5). This song actually quotes from that same chapter in the Bible, saying that a day is coming when the whole world will bow down on their knees and they will say that Jesus is Lord, that Jesus is God (Isaiah 45:23).

That phrase, "Jesus is Lord," was what people said when they wanted to become Christians, and back then they knew that this might get them killed. Others might put them to death because they didn't call Caesar Lord. Still, they confessed "Jesus is Lord" anyway. That's how much they believed in Jesus.

What does the title "Lord" mean? (*See if your child knows what the word means.*) This title tells us something about Jesus' relationship to God and something about His relationship to us. First, it means Jesus is equal to God the Father: both are God and both should be worshipped. Second, it means Jesus is our king and master and ruler. It means He owns us. We owe Him all of our obedience. He is king of our lives.

Questions for Your Kids:

1. What do you think it would be like if people wanted to kill you because of what you believed? (*See what your child says. Get your child to think about what he or she might do if someone came in your house while your family was reading the Bible and told you to stop worshiping Jesus. What would your child say?*)

2. Jesus has always been equal to God, but how did He get the title, "Lord"? (*Because Jesus was obedient to the Father, came to Earth, and died on the cross, the Father gave the Son the title "Lord." God the Son has always existed, but people didn't know it until Jesus came to Earth and did all of those amazing things. Now that Jesus has come, God the Father wants the world to honor Jesus by calling Him "Lord."*)

3. Why is "Lord" a good title for Jesus? (*It is a good title because it is a name God gives to Himself, and Jesus is God. It is also a good title because when we say, "Jesus is Lord," we are saying that He is the master of our lives and that we want to follow Him.*)

4. Do you sometime not act like Jesus is your Lord? (*Yes. Tell stories of the times when you don't obey Jesus. Have your child tell a story of his or her own. At the end make sure to say, "Even though we fail to obey God, the good news is that there's hope for people like us. If we are united to Christ, then we are forgiven for all of our sins, no matter how bad they are."*)

Prayer: "God, we confess with our mouth that Jesus is Lord (Romans 10:9). We believe You exalted Your Son Jesus and gave Him the name "Lord," the name above every name (Philippians 2:9). Forgive us for calling You Lord but not living like it. Amen."

LESSON 11: His Only Son

Opening Thought:

Do you know anyone who is adopted? (*See if you child can think of a friend who is adopted. Help your child if he or she can't think of anyone.*)

There are two ways to be somebody's son: you can be born into their family or you can be adopted. Adoption is when parents take a child who is not theirs, and they make that child legally their son or daughter. There are many children in the world who don't have moms and dads because their parents are dead or their parents abandoned them. Adoption is a way to give these kids a loving father and mother.

The Apostles' Creed says we believe in "Jesus Christ His only Son." What do think it means that Jesus is the Son of God? (*See what your child thinks about this question.*)

The words we're about to read were spoken by Jesus on the last night before His death. He is talking to His closest disciples about God the Father.

Scripture Reading: John 16:25-28 and 17:1-5

Explanation: Jesus prayed to His Father in heaven a lot, but on this occasion He prays out loud so His disciples can listen. He wants them to hear what He's saying to His Father, and while they are listening they learn something amazing.

In His prayer, Jesus says that before the world began, He was with the Father. He was in the Father's presence and was full of glory. Before He came to Earth as a man, before the world was even created, God the Father and God the Son were together. Even before time began, the Father has always loved the Son, and the Son has always trusted the Father.

Jesus knew His mission on Earth was finished and He was going back to the Father to enjoy that special glory again. Do you think Jesus was excited about that? (*See how your child responds to this and if he or she understands.*)

Jesus has a special relationship to the Father that no one else has. Think of it like human parents and their children. When a child is born, he looks like his parents because he has the same nature as them—he came from their bodies (*Give examples of child's own physical features or examples of other children your child knows*). But if those same parents adopt another child, they would love that child very much, but that child would not look like them because that child doesn't have the same nature. That second child came from different parents.

It is the same with Jesus. Jesus is God's Son by nature. We are God's children by adoption. The Bible calls Jesus God's only "begotten" Son: which mean He has the same nature as God the Father. They are both divine. They are both God. We are not God. We are God's creatures, but God adopts us into His family.

Do you know how God becomes our Father? (*See if your child can give an answer.*) Jesus tells us in the passage we just read. God adopts us into His family if we love His Son Jesus and if we believe Jesus came from God. Do you believe that? (*See how your child answers.*)

As Christians, we can pray to God as our Father. In this passage, Jesus tells his disciples how they should pray to God as Father. He tells them, "When you pray, don't pray to me. Don't ask me to talk to the Father for you. Talk directly to the Father yourself. He loves you. He has adopted you into His family."

Questions for Your Kids:

1. Jesus tells us we don't need to pray to Him but we can talk directly to the Father. How would it feel knowing that the God of the universe has adopted you? (*See how your child reacts to this idea.*)

2. Can you tell me: What is the difference between Jesus being God's Son and we being God's children? (*Jesus is God's Son by nature. They are both divine. God the Son has always been with the Father. We are God's children by adoption.*)

3. Can you remember what Jesus says here about becoming God's child. How did the first disciples become God's adopted children? (*They loved Jesus and believed He came from the Father.*)

4. Do you ever pray to God on your own? Has God ever answered one of your prayers? (*See if your child can give any examples. Give your child an example from your own life.*)

Prayer: "God, we believe that Jesus Christ is Your firstborn, the highest of the kings of the earth (Psalm 89:26-27). He is equal to You in every way (John 5:18). He is the radiance of Your glory (Hebrews 1:3). You sent Your only Son into the world that we might live through Him (1 John 4:9). Now we know that because You gave us Your greatest treasure, Your only Son, You will not hesitate to give us everything in the age to come (Romans 8:32). Help us to pray to You every day, remembering that You are our Father. Amen."

LESSON 12: Conceived and Born

Opening Thought:

How big is a baby when it is born? (*Have your child estimate how big an infant is. Perhaps tell your child how big he or she was at birth.*)

Some babies are born very tiny, just a few pounds. Other babies are born very large, maybe more than 10 pounds, but still that's small for a person.

Did you know that babies start out even smaller than that? How small do you think a baby is when it starts out? (*See if your child can estimate how small a newly conceived baby is.*)

A human baby is actually about a millimeter wide at the beginning. I can't even show you how little that is because it is so tiny. You wouldn't be able to see it with your eyes. When a baby is created in a mother's body, this is called "conception."

Do you know Jesus was also conceived? Did you know He started out life that small? In the Apostles' Creed, it says He was "conceived by the Holy Ghost" or sometimes called the Holy Spirit. This is what we'll be reading about Jesus today.

Scripture Reading: Luke 1:26-35

Explanation: Back then, girls got engaged to be married around the age of 12 or13, and that's probably how old Mary was when this event happened. Do you know anyone who is that age? (*Perhaps your child has a sibling or an acquaintance around that age.*)

One day a very special angel named Gabriel came to Mary. Gabriel was an important angel: about 500 years before this, God sent the angel Gabriel to a famous prophet named Daniel. Gabriel told Daniel all kind of things that would happen in the future, including the time when the Messiah, the Christ, would arrive. So now, Gabriel came back 500 years later to Mary because the time of the Messiah's birth was near.

Gabriel told Mary that she would conceive a son in her womb. This sounded very strange to Mary because she wasn't married to Joseph yet. Mary was betrothed to Joseph: this means they were legally bound to get married, but they hadn't had a wedding yet. You need to have a mom and a dad to have a baby, but Joseph couldn't be the baby's father, because they weren't married yet.

Gabriel told her that a miracle will take place. The Holy Spirit would surround Mary, and she would conceive a child without a human father. No child has ever been conceived this way!

Jesus came into the world the way we all did: born out of a woman. But how would Jesus be free from sin? Every person who has ever been born has come into the world as a sinner. Ever since our first parents, Adam and Eve, sinned and were punished by God, every person who has ever been born has come into the world with sin inside them. If Jesus was going to be born of a woman, how would He escape this?

He was born without sin because of the power of the Holy Spirit. Gabriel told Mary that after the Holy Spirit hovered over her and surrounded her that the child in her womb would be "holy." As far as His human nature goes, Jesus would be like Mary, but as far as sin goes, He would be like God who is totally without sin. This means Jesus was a human being like we are in every way, except He wasn't born sinful. This was all because of the power of the Holy Spirit.

Questions for Your Kids:

1. Did the Son of God exist before he was born to Mary? (*Yes. The Son of God is eternal just like God the Father and God the Holy Spirit.*)

2. How do we know that Jesus became a human being? How do we know He didn't just look like a human being? (*Because he was conceived inside the womb of a woman. Just like every baby, He started out very small and then took about 9 months to grow into a full-grown infant.*)

3. How was Jesus free from sin when He was born? (*Because the Holy Spirit made sure He was holy.*)

4. Jesus wasn't born sinful, but did He ever fall into sin after He was born? (*No. Jesus stayed sinless His entire life.*)

Prayer: "God, thank You for sending Your Son Jesus into the world. He was conceived at the perfect time in history, born of a woman (Galatians 4:4), born into the family of King David (Luke 1:32). We call Mary blessed because she got to be the mother of our Savior (Luke 1:46-48). He is the image of the invisible God (Colossians 1:15) who emptied Himself and came in human form (Philippians 2:7-8). Thank You that Jesus was like us in every way, except without sin (Hebrews 2:17; 4:15). Help us to look to Him when we are tempted, knowing that He understands what it is like to live in a sinful world. Amen."

LESSON 13: Suffered

Opening Thought:

Have you ever seen someone who is very poor? (*See if your child can think of anyone. Perhaps they met someone who was homeless or saw pictures of people who live in very poor places in the world.*)

There are places in the world where the average person has to live on a dollar or a couple dollars a day. That's not even enough to buy food for your family.

A lot of children in poor countries die from treatable problems like measles, malaria, or diarrhea. Sometimes, they have so little to eat, so little clean water to drink, and no doctors.

Today we're going to read about Jesus' life on the earth and how poor He was.

Scripture Reading: Matthew 8:16-27

Explanation: This episode in the Gospel of Matthew is a look into one day in the life of Jesus.

One evening, while Jesus was staying in the home of one of his disciples, people came to him who were sick and tormented by demons. Can you imagine what it was like? Maybe hundreds of people were pressing in around Jesus, all of them are sick in some way—coughing, sneezing, wheezing, unable to walk, bent over, covered in sores, crippled, and some unable to control themselves at all because demons had taken over their bodies. As the evening went on, it got darker and darker, but Jesus continued to heal everyone who came to Him.

Jesus came to rid the world of sickness, disease, pain, and death. Someday He's going to completely get rid of these things, and His miracles were a taste of that world to come.

It would have been a very exciting thing to watch as so many people were miraculously healed, but it also would have been exhausting for Jesus. In fact, after this Jesus decides to travel to the others side of the lake, and He is so tired, He is sleeping in the boat in the middle of a storm! He was exhausted from all the work He had done.

Why do you think Jesus was so tired? (*See what your child says.*) Jesus was probably physically tired because He had stayed up late into the evening healing lots of people. He was also probably emotionally exhausted—He had just stared into the sad faces of hundreds of people who were sick and dying. He shared their sadness. He had compassion on them. He shared their joy when they were completely healed.

Some people are so amazed by Jesus, they can't wait to be one of His disciples and follow Him. One man was a scribe, which means he probably was wealthier than most people. When he said, "Teacher, I want to follow you wherever you go," Jesus replied to him, "Foxes have holes, and birds have nests, but the Son of Man has nowhere to lay His head." The title "Son of Man" was Jesus' favorite title for Himself—He called Himself the Son of Man all the time. Jesus is telling this man, "You say you'll follow me wherever I go? Just remember, I don't even have a home to live in. Are you willing to leave all the comforts of your home to follow me?" Would you have still followed Jesus? (*See how your child reacts to the idea of having no home.*)

Jesus didn't have a lot of money in His life. He was born in an animal stall instead of a house. He lived in a small village called Nazareth, surrounded by poor farmers. He worked a manual labor job. During His ministry, He stayed in other people's homes or slept outside on the ground. He depended on the hospitality of others. He owned very little. Even at the end of His life, He was buried in a borrowed tomb.

In the Apostles' Creed, we say that we believe Jesus "suffered." He didn't just suffer at the end of His life. He suffered His entire life. He was born into a poor family, surrounded by poor and suffering people, and lived a very meager life. He didn't come expecting to be treated like royalty—even though that's what He deserved as the Son of God. He came from the riches of heaven into the depths of human poverty.

Questions for Your Kids:

1. Why do you think Jesus spent all that time healing everyone? (*There are a couple reasons. First, Jesus had compassion on them. He felt bad for them in their suffering, and He wanted to help them. Second, Jesus was giving them a preview of His kingdom that is coming. He was showing them His power.*)

2. He was the Son of God. Do you think He got tired and hungry? (*Yes. In this story He's so tired He's sleeping on a boat in the middle of a storm. We know He got hungry, thirsty, and felt all the aches and pains we all feel in life.*)

3. Why do you think Jesus was born into such a poor life? (*He experienced all the sufferings of this world. Now, when we pray to God, we know that Jesus understands all the troubles we experience in this life because He experienced them Himself.*)

Prayer: "God, though Your Son was rich, for our sakes He became poor so that we in our poverty could become rich (2 Corinthians 8:9). He took the form of a servant (Philippians 2:7). He was a man of sorrows and acquainted with grief (Isaiah 53:3). He became like us in every respect so that He could become our merciful and faithful high priest in heaven (Hebrews 2:17). Lord, help us not to be afraid to follow Jesus, even if it means giving up the comforts of this life. Amen."

LESSON 14:
Under Pontius Pilate

Opening Thought:

In the Apostles' Creed, there are only a few people mentioned by name. Of course it mentions God the Father, Jesus Christ, and the Holy Ghost. It also mentions Jesus' mother. Do you remember her name? (*Mary*)

But there's one more person mentioned right after Mary. Can you think of who it is? (*Pontius Pilate*)

The Apostles' Creed says Jesus "suffered under Pontius Pilate." Pilate was the governor of Judea when Jesus was crucified. Why would the authors of the Apostles' Creed put his name in there? (*See if your child can think of any reasons.*)

Let's read the story about Pontius Pilate from the Gospel of Mark.

Scripture Reading: Mark 15:1-15

Explanation: There are two things Pontius Pilate's name in the Creed tells us. First, it tells us *where* Jesus died. Pilate was governor of the Roman province of Judea, which is in Israel. Pilate's name also tells us *when* Jesus died. According to Roman historians, Pilate was governor of Judea from 26 to 36 AD. This means Jesus died some time between these dates. That was about 2,000 years ago.

There are some people out there who think the stories about Jesus are just made up stories. But by putting Pilate's name in this Creed, Christians were telling the world that Jesus was real: He lived and died in a real place, and we even know when He lived. It didn't just happen like in a fairy tale: a long time ago in a land far, far away. Jesus was a real person.

Another thing Pilate's name reminds us about it Jesus' trial before He was killed. The Jewish leaders wanted to Jesus to die, but they didn't have the authority to kill Him. Only the Roman governor could order that someone be executed, so the Jewish leaders brought Jesus to the governor, Pontius Pilate.

The story is clear: Pilate believes Jesus is innocent—certainly not deserving of death—but the Jewish leaders want Him to die. It was during the feast of Passover, and Pilate usually let the people choose a famous prisoner to be released. He gave them a choice: release Jesus, the one who calls Himself the King, or release Barabbas, a murderer and rebel against the government. The people chose Barabbas instead of Jesus, showing just how badly they wanted Jesus to die.

Pilate is amazed at Jesus. Other people who came before him trembled with fear, begging to be set free or trying to convince him that they are innocent. Not Jesus. Jesus says only a few words to Pilate, and the rest of the time He is quiet and confident.

Why do you think Pilate sentenced Jesus to die if he really believed Jesus was innocent? (*See if your child can come up with any ideas. If they can't think of anything, read verse 15 again and see if that helps.*)

Pilate condemns Jesus to die because he doesn't want to cause a problem between himself and the Jewish leaders. You see, Pilate had offended the Jews greatly in the past, and they had reported him to the Emperor. He didn't want to get in trouble again, so he finally gave in and gave the people what they wanted.

Here's the strangest thing about this story: Jesus is the real ruler, the real king of the whole world, and He's being condemned by a temporary human ruler. Jesus is the one who will return some day and be judge of the whole world, and He's being judged by a human judge. Jesus is the perfect Judge, and He's being judged by someone who isn't fair at all.

Questions to Ask Your Kids:

1. Let's see if you remember: when was Pontius Pilate the governor of Judea? (*Between 26 and 36 AD*)

2. Why is it good that Pilate's name is in the Creed? (*Because it reminds us that Jesus really lived at a certain time and lived in a certain place.*)

3. Why did Pilate condemn Jesus to die? (*He wanted to please the crowds so he didn't get in trouble.*)

4. Why do you think Jesus wasn't afraid of Pilate? (*Jesus trusted His Father. He knew He was going to die on a cross, so He knew it was part of His Father's plan to be judged.*)

5. What was Jesus' confession before Pilate? When He did speak, what did He say? *(If your child can't remember, read verse 2 again. Jesus said that He was the King of the Jews.)*

Prayer: "God, thank You for the faithfulness of Jesus. When He was hated by His own people, He did not hate them back. When He was on trial, He did not threaten anyone. Instead He entrusted Himself to You, the true Judge (1 Peter 2:23). Help us to be like Him. Help us to remember the good confession Jesus made before Pilate and give us the bravery to speak the truth like Jesus did, even if it costs us our life like it did Jesus' (1 Timothy 6:13). Amen."

LESSON 15: Crucified (Part 1)

Opening Thought:

What we're going to talk about today can be very sad. We're going to talk about how Jesus died. What do you know about that? (*See how much your child knows already.*)

In Israel, where Jesus lived, after someone was put to death, sometimes they would hang that person's body on a tree or a wooden post so that anyone who walked by would see them and remember the terrible crime they committed. God's law in the Old Testament said that anyone who was hanged on a tree or a wooden pole was "cursed" by God because of the awful sins they did.

When Jesus died, he wasn't just hung up on wood *after* He died. He actually died by being nailed to a wooden cross. When the people walked by and saw Him, they probably thought, "That man is cursed by God for his sins." Let's read about what happened.

Scripture Reading: Matthew 27:26-43

Explanation: Crucifixion is one of the most terrible forms of execution ever created by human beings. Good citizens of the Roman Empire thought it was rude to even speak of it, because it was so terrible—something for the worst criminals.

Early in the morning, after His trial before Pontius Pilate, he was scourged. This means His arms were tied or chained above his head to a post while soldiers took a special leather whip with multiple lashes in it and beat his back. These lashes usually contained small pieces of bone and metal, so when the whip struck His back, it would tear through His skin. Some prisoners who experienced this would pass out from the pain. Can you imagine that?

Then the soldiers mocked Him. A whole battalion of soldiers—possibly up to 600 men—made fun of Him. They twisted together thorns into the shape of crown and pressed it on to Jesus' head, piercing His scalp. They bowed down in front of Him, pretending He was a king while they teased Him. They punched Him, spit in His face, and hit Him with a wooden reed. Why do you think they were so cruel? (*See how your child reacts.*)

After this, Jesus was forced to carry a large beam of wood, probably weighing over 75 pounds, but He was so weakened by His beating, they had to ask another man to help Him. He walked outside the city to a place called Golgotha, which was a place they killed criminals.

They laid Him on his back, stretched out His arms, and nailed His wrists to the beam of wood using 7-inch (18-cm) spikes. This would have been extremely painful, sending shooting pain through His arms and back. After this they lifted the beam of wood up in the air and attached it to a long wooden post. Then they nailed His feet to the post.

Jesus hung on the cross for six hours. It would have been very hard to breathe in that position. Jesus was in pain all over His body.

The soldiers hung something called a titulus above his head. When criminals were crucified, the titulus was a sign that had the person's name and the crime for which they were guilty. Jesus' titulus said, "This is Jesus of Nazareth, the King of the Jews." This was what they thought Jesus' crime was: claiming to be the Messiah.

The thing was: Jesus really *is* the Messiah. He wasn't guilty of any crime or any sin. So why was God letting Jesus die this way? God's law said everyone hung on a piece of wood or a tree was cursed by God. Was God cursing His own Son by having Him die on the cross? (*See how your child responds to this.*)

Actually, the Bible says Jesus was cursed by His Father, but it wasn't because He had sinned. Galatians 3:13 says Jesus became a curse *for us*. He died in the most cursed way possible because God wanted to give us an important message: Jesus rescues us from God's curse against sin. He was cursed by God for *our sin*.

Questions for Your Kids:

1. Do we all deserve to be cursed by God for our sin? (*Yes. Every person is sinful.*)

2. Did Jesus deserve God's curse? (*No. Jesus was sinless. He never did anything wrong.*)

3. Why did God allow the Jewish leaders to hand Jesus over to the Romans who executed Him in the most painful, shameful way possible? (*Jesus chose to follow the Father's plan to come to Earth and take the curse of sin upon Himself. He took our punishment for us. God took the curse off us and put it on His Son Jesus.*)

Prayer: "Thank You, God, that Christ died for our sins, just like the Scriptures said He would (1 Corinthians 15:3). He redeemed us from the curse of the law by becoming a cure for us (Galatians 3:13). He bore our sin in His body on the cross. By His wounds we are healed (1 Peter 2:24). Help us to think about the cross, not just as something painful that happened to Jesus, but as something that took away our sin. Amen."

LESSON 16: Crucified (Part 2)

Opening Thought:

What do you remember from the last lesson about the crucifixion of Jesus? Do you remember what He went through? (*See if your child can remember any specific events: how Jesus was beaten, whipped, mocked, made to carry His cross, nailed to the wood, etc.*)

Remember, Jesus told people He was God's Messiah, the Son of God, the Savior, but there He was hanging on a cross dying. How could He be the one God sent if He was dying a shameful and miserable death? If He really was the Son of God, wouldn't the Father protect Him?

Today, we're going to finish the story of the crucifixion and hear from Jesus' own lips the kind of pain He went through on the cross.

Scripture Reading: Mark 15:33-39

Explanation: The Apostles' Creed says Jesus Christ was "crucified, dead, and buried." They nailed Him to the cross at 9:00 in the morning. Around noon, after three long hours, a mysterious darkness covered the land.

Three more hours passed in darkness, and finally, around 3:00 in the afternoon Jesus cried out in a loud voice, "My God, My God, why have you forsaken me?" Had God really abandoned Jesus on the cross?

Remember, last time we talked about how Jesus was *cursed* by His Father. Even though His Father loved Him, and even though Jesus wasn't guilty of any sin, He knew the Father's plan was to put the sins of the world on Him. When Jesus died on the cross, He would experience God's great anger at sin—as if He were a sinner. God would turn His face away from Jesus and let Him suffer and die.

Can you imagine what this was like for Jesus? He had known and been with His Father forever: even before He was born, He was with His Father. But at this one time in history, the Father would totally turn away from the Son. Why did God do this? (*See how your child reacts to this idea.*)

The reason that the Father and the Son did this is so that we would never have to experience God's anger ourselves. This is how God forgives. Before Jesus, God's people made animal sacrifices. They would take their goat or sheep or ram or bull into a temple, they would confess their sins, and a priest would kill the animal. That person knew the animal was dying for his sins. God was turning his anger away from the person and putting it on the animal.

When Jesus came, He came to be the perfect sacrifice, the final sacrifice. No matter how many times you sacrificed an animal, you still kept on sinning, so you'd have to sacrifice more animals. But Jesus was the greatest sacrifice. Because He is the Son of God—because He is so perfect and so loved by the Father—His sacrifice is worth more than all the animals in the world. When He died, He died for all of our sins: all of our sins from the past, all our sins right now, and all of our sins in the future.

Jesus is able to save all who come to Him. He takes away our sin. God doesn't treat us like His enemy anymore, but instead treats us like His children.

Questions for Your Kids:

1. Have you ever felt like God was absent, like He wasn't there? (*See what your child says to this question.*)

2. What do you think that was like for Jesus to feel totally forsaken by His Father? (*See if your child can comprehend what it would be like.*)

3. If every time you sinned you had to kill and sacrifice an animal, how do you think that would feel? (*It would make you think twice before you sinned because you would realize how terrible sin is. The wages of sin is death, and if every time you saw an animal die for your sin, you would remember that sin is really awful.*)

4. What do you think was more painful: the nails in Jesus' hands or feeling like His Father was forsaking Him? (*His Father forsaking Him on the cross would have been terribly painful.*)

Prayer: "Father, all have sinned and fall short of Your glory, but You have given us grace through Jesus Christ. He atoned for our sins on the cross (Romans 3:23-25). The animal sacrifices of the past all pointed forward to the day when Christ, the perfect sacrifice, would come. His blood gives us eternal redemption (Hebrews 9:11-14). Help us to never forget the great price He paid for our sins. Amen."

LESSON 17: Dead & Buried

Opening Thought:

Roman soldiers in the time of Christ performed a lot of crucifixions. They crucified criminals on crosses all the time. They became experts at death.

What was surprising about Jesus' death is that it only took six hours. Sometimes people would stay alive on their crosses for several days. In fact, there were two criminals being crucified at the same time as Jesus, one on his right, and the other on his left, and they were still alive when Jesus died.

If you wanted to check to see if someone was alive or dead, how would you check? (*You could check someone's heartbeat. Show your child how to check his or her own pulse. You could check to see if someone is breathing. Have your child feel his or her own breath.*)

The soldiers made sure Jesus was dead in their own way. Let's read about that.

Scripture Reading: John 19:28-42

Explanation: The Apostles' Creed says Jesus was "crucified, dead, and buried," and that's what this text talks about.

Jesus was crucified during the holy feast of Passover, and the Jewish people didn't want the bodies of those being crucified hanging up on the crosses, so they decided to speed up their deaths. They went to the criminals on Jesus' right and left and broke their legs. This made it almost impossible for them to breath, so they quickly died.

They noticed Jesus was already dead, so they didn't break His legs, but they made sure He was dead by taking a long spear and pierced His side. The text here says that one of Jesus' disciples saw this happen with his own eyes so that we would know it was really true. When the spear entered Jesus' side, water and blood flowed out of the wound. If there was any doubt that Jesus was dead, when they drove that spear into His side, the soldiers knew for sure.

Two men asked for permission to take Jesus' body, and they buried Him in a tomb made of rock. They wrapped his body in a linen shroud and brought spices to put on Jesus' body. This was very expensive. Not everyone could afford to be buried in a tomb all alone or had many pounds of spices for their burial. But these men wanted to honor Jesus.

These stories show us that Jesus really was dead when His body came down from the cross. The soldiers made sure of it, and the men who took Jesus' body could see it—this is why they buried Him.

Questions for Your Kids:

1. Why is it so important to believe that Jesus was completely dead and not just hurt or weak when He came down from the cross? (*Because later Jesus is going to be raised from the dead by the power of God. If He never really died, then His resurrection never happened.*)

2. In another Bible story we learn that the Jewish leaders had armed guards stationed around Jesus' tomb after He was buried. They didn't want anyone stealing Jesus' body. Why do you think they did that? (*Jesus had claimed that He would rise from the dead. The Jewish leaders didn't believe it would happen, but they were afraid someone would steal the body and then lie about Jesus rising from the dead. The guards around Jesus' tomb were there to make sure no one got in or out.*)

2. It says in this text that the men who buried Jesus were His disciples, but they were secret disciples—they didn't want other people to know that they followed Jesus. Why do you think they were scared to tell people? (*Some people hated Jesus. That's why they had Jesus killed. These men didn't want others to know they were disciples because they didn't want to be hated, too.*)

Prayer: "God, you have given us many proofs that Jesus really died on the cross so that we can believe in His resurrection. Thank you that Jesus' tomb is empty today. Help us not to be afraid of what others might think of us because we follow Jesus. Help us to tell others that we are His disciples, His followers. Amen."

LESSON 18:
Descendit Ad Inferna

Opening Thought:

We've been talking about the death of Jesus. What do you think happens after you die? When you breathe your last breath, what happens to you next? (*See what your child thinks about this.*)

The Bible says we're more than just a body. We also have a soul. When we die, while our bodies stay here on Earth, our souls go on to live somewhere else. Those who have been forgiven of all their sins go to a place the Bible calls Paradise, which means a pleasant garden. It is the same word used to describe the Garden of Eden, the perfect world God made in the very beginning before anyone ever sinned.

Those who have not been forgiven of their sins go to a place of suffering where they wait to be judged.

The Apostles' Creed says Jesus descended into hell after He died. The word "hell" may not be the best translation anymore, because today that word gives people the idea that Jesus died and went to a place of punishment. That isn't true. "Hell" is an older English word that is a translation of the Latin word *inferna*, which means a lower region, the underworld. Let's read what the Bible says about that.

Scripture Reading: Luke 23:39-46

Explanation: Two criminals were crucified along with Jesus, one on His right and the other on His left. One of the criminals wanted to be rescued from the cross. The other one was different. He feared God. He knew he was being punished for his sins. He also believed that Jesus was innocent and that He was the true king. The criminal doesn't ask to be rescued from the cross. He asks Jesus to remember Him when He comes into His kingdom.

Jesus knew they both were going to die that day, and He made an amazing promise to the criminal: "Today, you'll be with me in Paradise."

There are two important things to remember when we think about Jesus' soul leaving His body. First, when we say Jesus descended into hell, we're saying that Jesus really died a human death. Like all human beings, Jesus experienced a complete death—His soul was separated from His body. When Jesus prayed on the cross, He said, "Father, into Your hands I commit my spirit." He gave up His spirit and died.

Second, when we say Jesus descended into hell, we're saying that He went to the land of the dead, not as a prisoner, but as a victor. He went to Paradise to be with that criminal and any other faithful believers who died before them. What an amazing day that must have been for all those people, to finally meet the Messiah, to meet the One who died for their sins. But Jesus was only there to stay for three days, and then He would rise from the dead.

Questions for Your Kids:

1. Often when people think about death, it can be a scary thing because they aren't sure what comes after this life. Have you ever thought about what will happen after you die? (*See what your child says about his or her own fears, worries, or anticipations.*)

2. If we really believe Jesus went to Paradise after He died, how does this comfort us when we think about our own death? (*Because we know that Jesus has experienced death before us, we know that if we believe in Jesus, we have nothing to fear.*)

3. Did Jesus stay in Paradise? (*No. Three days later he rose from the dead.*)

4. We don't know much about the criminals who died on the crosses next to Jesus, but one of them went to Paradise after He died. What do we know about that man and what he believed? (*We know he was a criminal who was being punished for a great crime. We know he believed he deserved his punishment. We also know that he feared God: he knew God was his judge. We know he heard that Jesus was the Messiah, and he believed it was true. We also know that he believed Jesus was innocent and that He was going to His kingdom after He died.*

Prayer: "God, thank You for sending Jesus to die for us. By dying, He destroyed the power of the devil, the one who has the power of death. Jesus sets us free from the fear of death (Hebrews 2:14-15). We look forward to Paradise, to eat from the tree of life once again (Revelation 2:7). Give us faith like the criminal on the cross, who trusted Jesus to bring us into His kingdom. Amen."

LESSON 19: He Arose (Part 1)

Opening Thought:

Let's say you were a police officer and you got a call to go to the scene of a car accident. You got there and made sure the drivers of the cars were okay, and then you started asking them what happened. The first guy says, "It wasn't my fault! It was the other guy's fault!" The second driver says, "No! He's the one who hit me!" After listening to them argue, you think, "There has to be a way to find out what really happened." How could you find that out? (*See if your child comes up with anything. Ask your child, "What if there were other people standing around who saw the accident?"*)

If there were other people who saw the accident, you could talk to each of them. What if there were lots of people who saw it? You could go up to each of them, one by one, and ask them what happened, and what if they each told you the same story: it was the second driver who was at fault? What if at the end of a long day you've interviewed hundreds of people, and they all say the same thing about what they saw? It would be pretty easy to decide what happened, wouldn't it?

Today we're going to read about something that hundreds of people witnessed—one of the most important events in history.

Scripture Reading: 1 Corinthians 15:3-8

Explanation: The author, Paul, is reminding his readers about the gospel, the good news. He says, "Remember what I taught you when I came to visit you." He says that Jesus died, was buried, and then on the third day after He died, He rose from the dead. But he doesn't stop there. He says Jesus was actually seen by not one, not a few, but hundreds of people.

It would be easy to think Jesus' resurrection was just a made up story, wouldn't it? After all, people don't just rise from the dead every day. It seems like an unbelievable story. But Paul knew it was real, and he tells them why.

He says there were some very important church leaders who saw Jesus alive after He died. He mentions Cephas, which was another name for the apostle Peter. He mentions James, Jesus' brother, who led the church in Jerusalem. He mentions that Jesus appeared to the twelve apostles: these were twelve special men that Jesus selected to lead His church. He mentions that all the apostles saw Jesus—this is an even bigger group of people who later went out to preach about Jesus.

Then Paul says that more than 500 people saw Jesus at the same time. He even says that, at the time he wrote this letter, most of them were still alive. Just like in the story of the car accident, what if you decided to interview all of those people? One by one you asked them about the times they saw Jesus alive. You talk to Peter, James, all the apostles, and then hundreds of others. At the end of all those conversations there wouldn't be a doubt in your mind: Jesus really did rise from the dead!

Paul also writes that he was a witness of the resurrection. It happened quite a while after the others saw Jesus, but he really did see Jesus. The thing that's important to remember about Paul is that he wasn't even a Christian when he saw Jesus. In fact, he hated Christians. He thought they were all telling lies. He wanted to see them all arrested and thrown in prison, or even killed. One day, while he was on his way to arrest Christians, Jesus suddenly appeared to him. A blinding light surrounded him, and he heard the voice of Christ tell him that he wasn't going to fight Christians anymore; instead he was going to preach about Christ.

There's a line in the Apostles' Creed that says, "The third day He arose again from the dead." When we say that, we should remember that God gave them many convincing proofs that Jesus was really alive, because so many people saw Him alive.

Questions for Your Kids:

1. What would it have been like to know that Jesus died a horrible death on the cross but then see Him alive again with your own eyes? (*Get your child talking about how exciting or confusing it would have been.*)

2. As the first few people saw Jesus alive, do you think it was easy for others to believe them when they told the story? (*No. Many of them doubted. If you read the stories, no one believed the first women who saw Jesus. Even when whole groups of people started seeing Jesus, others doubted them. No one had ever seen anything like it before, so it was hard to believe at first.*)

3. Is it possible that all those people were just lying? (*No. These people went on to tell others about Jesus, and many of them suffered and died for it. Why would that many people die for something they knew was a lie?*)

Prayer: "God, thank you for bringing Jesus up from the dead. This was to fulfill what was written about Jesus in the prophets long before He came (Luke 24:44). Thank You that You gave Your disciples many convincing proofs that You were alive, appearing to them over and over again (Acts 1:3). Blessed are those who have not seen Jesus but still believe (John 20:29). Give us faith to believe in the resurrection. Amen."

LESSON 20: He Arose (Part 2)

Opening Thought:

We've been talking a lot about Jesus and what He did in His life. But did Jesus ever sin? (*No. Jesus never did anything to offend His Father. He always followed God's law.*)

He never sinned but He was surrounded by sin, wasn't He? He grew up in a sinful family. He had sinful friends. He also lived in a world with the effects of sin all around Him. Everywhere He looked, He saw pain and sickness and death. He saw friends and family die.

Was Jesus ever tempted to sin? (*Yes. He never gave into temptation, either in his actions or in His desires, but He was tempted by the devil and the world.*)

Every moment of Jesus' life, He had to make the choice to obey His Father or sin, and He always chose to obey God. Then, at the very end of His life, He chose to obey the Father's plan and die on the cross, even though it was very painful.

The good news is that after Jesus died and rose again, He was free from this sinful world. Let's read about that.

Scripture Reading: Romans 6:6-11

Explanation: The Apostles' Creed says, "The third day He arose again from the dead." This doesn't mean that Jesus' body was exactly the same as it was before. It was the same body, but there was something different about it. Now, Jesus can never die again. His body is no longer weak, but glorious and powerful. Sin has absolutely no power in Jesus' life, and death cannot touch Him.

The Bible promises that one day the whole world will live like Jesus is living right now. One day this whole world will be renewed, and death will be gone for good.

Until that day, we have a very special gift from God. If we really believe in Christ, then the Spirit of Christ actually lives inside us. We belong to God. Remember how powerful Jesus is now. Because His Spirit lives inside us, He gives us power to say "no" to temptation just like He said "no." We are still living in a sinful world and we are still living in weak bodies. We are still surrounded by sin. But if the Spirit of Christ is in us, sin doesn't have power over us anymore. We have the power to live a new life.

This passage says Christ is *dead to sin*—which means sin has no power over Him. This passage also says *we* are dead to sin because Christ lives in us. The same power that raised Jesus from the dead is inside us. How powerful is that? Powerful enough to raise the dead; powerful enough to transform Jesus' body into something that will never die; powerful enough to completely transform the whole world at the end of time and get rid of death forever: that's the kind of power that is in everyone who is a true Christian.

Is that powerful enough to help you overcome temptations? (*Yes.*)

Is that powerful enough to kill the sin inside you? (*Yes.*)

This passage says we need to consider ourselves already dead to sin. That means we need to remember this every day. When you feel like sinning, you say to yourself, "No, this is not who I really am. I belong to God. Sin doesn't have power over me. I have resurrection power inside me."

Questions for Your Kids:

1. Let's think about Jesus' resurrection for a minute. How was Jesus' body the same as before He died? (*It was the same body. When Jesus rose from the dead, His tomb was empty. His body rose up.*)

2. How was Jesus' body different? (*It wasn't weak anymore, but powerful. He couldn't die anymore. His body was full of glory.*)

3. What does it means that Jesus is dead to sin? (*Christ never sinned, but He did live in a sinful world. He doesn't live in this sinful world anymore. He can't be tempted to sin. He'll never feel the consequences of sin again.*)

4. Why are Christians dead to sin? (*Because the Spirit of Christ lives inside them. He gives them power to overcome temptation and sin.*)

Prayer: "God, thank You that we are raised with Christ. By grace we have been saved (Ephesians 2:5-6). Help us to set our minds and hearts on things above, where Christ is seated at Your right hand (Colossians 3:1-2). We have a living hope because of the resurrection of Jesus Christ (1 Peter 1:3). Thank You for uniting us to Him. Help us to walk in the freedom from sin because of the power of His resurrection. Amen."

LESSON 21: He Ascended

Opening Thought:

How many times do you think Jesus appeared to His disciples after He rose from the dead? *(See how many your child guesses.)*

The New Testament doesn't say how many times, but there were at least ten times, and possibly many more. We know He appeared to a group of women near His tomb. He appeared to a woman named Mary Magdalene. He appeared to one of His chief disciples Peter. He appeared to a couple disciples while walking on a road from Jerusalem. He appeared to his main group of disciples on several occasions. He appeared to his brother James. He appeared to a crowd of 500 people on one occasion.

He also appeared to them 40 days after He rose from the dead. That's what we're going to read about today.

Scripture Reading: Acts 1:1-12

Explanation: Can you imagine what this was like for these disciples? Jesus has taken them to the side of a mountain called the Mount of Olives. This place had been a favorite spot for Jesus and His closest disciples. They had spent many nights there. Jesus had several important conversations with His disciples there on that mountain.

He tells them to go back and stay in the city of Jerusalem, only a short walk away, and wait for a special gift from heaven: the gift of God's Holy Spirit. The Spirit was going to give them power to carry out their special mission. But why would they need the Holy Spirit? Wasn't Jesus going to be there to help them?

Suddenly, as Jesus was speaking, He started to rise into the sky. Can you picture the look on their faces? They had seen Jesus do some amazing things during His ministry: they saw Him heal hundreds of people, cast our demons, walk on water, and many other miracles, but there on the side of the mountain, they saw Him start to fly into the sky! Suddenly a cloud came and surrounded Him, and took Him away like a chariot takes away a victorious warrior. And there they stood on the grass staring into the sky. That was the last time they all saw Jesus together.

God was teaching Jesus' disciples something important. The Father was welcoming Jesus home. The Father was giving His Son great honor again as the bright clouds of God's glory surrounded Him.

The Father was also giving them a preview of the future. Remember what happened right after Jesus ascended into heaven? Two men in white robes—two angels—suddenly appeared on the mountain, telling the disciples that Jesus was going to come back the same way He went into heaven. Some day, the clouds of God's glory will appear again and bring Jesus back down to Earth. Some day—and it may not be long—Jesus will come back down, and when He does, He will transform the whole world into His kingdom.

In the Apostles' Creed, when we say, "He ascended into heaven," remember what that really means: His disciples actually saw Him rise up into the sky, saw Him glorified and honored by the Father, and heard the great promise that someday Jesus is going to come back the same way.

Questions for Your Kids:

1. We know a little about what it looked like for the disciples that day. But what do you think it looked like to the angels in heaven when Jesus came back? (*Have your kids imagine it. Jesus was known in heaven as God the Son, their Creator, but He had been gone for more than 30 years while He lived on Earth. Suddenly Jesus comes up, surrounded by God's glory, raised from the dead in a glorious, perfect body. He was coming back not just as God the Son, but also as a man. The angels must have been amazed!*)

2. How long did Jesus stay on the earth appearing to His disciples? (*40 days*)

3. Will Jesus come back to Earth some day? (*Yes. He's going to come down the same way He went up. He will be riding on the clouds and come back down to Earth, and we will get a chance to see Him with our own eyes.*)

4. Do we know when Jesus will come back? (*No. The Bible tells us about Jesus' return, but doesn't tell us the day He will return. We need to be ready at all times.*)

Prayer: "God, thank You for glorifying and honoring Your Son by taking Him home to be with You. He was taken up in glory (1 Timothy 3:16). He ascended into heaven that He might fulfill all things (Ephesians 4:10). You have given Christ a name that is above every name, and someday every knee will bow and every mouth will confess that Jesus Christ is Lord (Philippians 2:9). It is all to Your glory, God. Help us to honor Jesus just as You do. Amen."

LESSON 22: God's Right Hand

Opening Thought:

Long ago, if you were a great and powerful king, there would be many important people in your palace who would help you rule your kingdom. You would have advisors who would help you make decisions. You would have servants. You would have generals and military leaders to help you command your armies. Who else would you have in your palace? (*See what your children think of.*)

But you would also have someone who sat at your right hand. To sit at someone's right hand meant that person was your most trusted advisor, your second-in-command, the one you love. The right hand of the king was the most honored position in the whole kingdom.

In the Apostles' Creed we read that Jesus sat down at "the right hand of God." Let's read a passage about that.

Scripture Reading: Romans 8:31-39

Explanation: The whole point of this passage is that if we belong to God, then we should feel secure in how much God loves us. What is a reason we might doubt that God loves us? Can you think of a reason? (*See if your child can think of anything.*)

Think of all the bad things that can happen to us in life. Paul, the author, lists many of them out here, and these are all things he experienced in his own life: we can be in distress, we can have various trials in life, we can get really hungry and be without food for a time, we could find ourselves in great danger, people can be against us, they can accuse us of doing bad things—even if we didn't do them—we could be persecuted for being a Christian, or we could even be killed for being a Christian. With all these bad things that could happen to us, it would be easy to forget the most important thing: God loves us and nothing can change that.

We know nothing can change that because of what Christ has done for us. Paul writes here that Christ is at the right hand of the Father. God is the great ruler of the universe, and right now, as we speak, Jesus Christ is sitting at His right hand ruling the universe with Him. He is in complete control. Even when bad things happen to us, Jesus never loses control of anything.

This is even true when we feel guilty about something. Let's say you do something bad and you feel guilty about it, or let's say somebody else accuses you of doing something bad, even though you didn't do it. You might start to feel really bad, wouldn't you? Whether you feel really guilty because you did something wrong, or whether others are trying to make you feel bad by saying you did something wrong, we have to remember something very important: there is only one Judge who really matters. People who accuse you aren't your judges. You aren't even your own judge. Only God is your judge.

And what has that great Judge already said about you? This passage says if you are a child of God, God has already *justified* you. This means God says, "Jesus has died for you. He has already paid the price for your sins. I don't see you as guilty anymore." Other people might hate you because they think you did something bad. You might even feel really bad about something you did. But God says, "I don't condemn you. You are my child."

Right now, Jesus is at God's right hand, and do you know what He's doing there? He's praying for us. Right now, He is sitting there and the Father can see the holes in Jesus' hands and feet where the nails used to be. He can see the hole in Jesus' side where He was pierced. As Jesus prays, He is always defending us before the Father. When people in the world accuse us, when we accuse ourselves, or when Satan himself accuses us, Jesus prays, "I have died for their sins. You put the curse of their sin on Me on the cross. They are forgiven." The Father always hears Jesus' prayer because Jesus is at His right hand: the Father never gets tired of hearing that prayer because He loves Jesus more than anything in the world.

Questions for Your Kids:

1. How does it make you feel knowing that Jesus is praying for us? (*See how your child reacts to this idea. Does he or she feel confused? Joy?*)

2. What does it mean that Jesus is sitting at God's right hand? (*It means Jesus is the most honored position in the whole universe. It means Jesus' is ruling the universe with the Father as a king. It means Jesus is praying for us to the Father all the time.*)

3. When we feel guilty because of something we did wrong, what should we remember? (*We should remember that Jesus doesn't condemn us or treat us like His enemy. The Father doesn't condemn us or treat us like His enemy. Jesus is praying for us, saying that we are forgiven.*)

Prayer: "God, it is wonderful to know that Jesus is at Your right hand. (Matthew 28:18-20). You have given all authority in heaven and on Earth to Him, and He is honored above everyone and everything (Psalm 110:1). He is in complete control of all that happens to us. We love knowing that You hear and answer every prayer He prays for us, and because of this we know we will ultimately be saved from all the evil in this world (Hebrews 7:25). If we sin, we know He is our advocate because He died for our sins (1 John 2:1-2). When our hearts condemn us, helps us to remember that You are greater than our hearts. Amen."

LESSON 23: Coming to Judge

Opening Thought:

Imagine you committed a crime. Can you think of a crime that some people commit? (*Have your child think of a crime like stealing or killing.*)

What if you got caught committing this crime and needed to be taken to a courtroom so you could stand in front of a judge? That might be kind of scary thinking about what the judge might say. What punishment will he give you? (*Have your child think of what an appropriate sentence would be.*)

Imagine the large courtroom filled with people—all staring at you. At the front is a big bench that's on a platform. The judge walks in wearing a dark robe. He sits down at the bench and bangs his gavel, making a loud cracking noise. Then he hears about the crime you've committed. Suddenly he says in a loud voice: "Guilty!" How do you think you would feel? (*See how your child reacts to this idea.*)

In the Apostles' Creed, it says Jesus "will come to judge the quick and the dead." This means when Jesus comes back, He'll judge everyone who is alive at that time and everyone who has ever lived before. Let's read about this.

Scripture Reading: Revelation 20:11-15

Explanation: The One seated on this throne is so amazing, so beautiful, so startling, the author doesn't even describe Him. He is so amazing, when He appears the earth and the sky flee away. All of God's creation comes unraveled, and the only things that are left are Jesus and billions and billion of people, all standing before His great, white throne.

The Bible says everyone who has ever lived, great and small, will stand there. It doesn't matter if the person was the poorest beggar who ever lived or the richest king. Everyone is standing there in front of Jesus, the judge of the whole world.

This passage talks about books that Jesus has. In these books is everything that Jesus knows about us. How much does Jesus know about us? (*He knows about everything we've ever done, said, or thought. He knows things about us we don't even know about ourselves. He knows everything about us.*)

God remembers all the stuff we've ever done. Sometimes people do good things that glorify God, but many things people do are evil. Sometimes we can even do something that looks good, but we're only doing it to make people like us or we're only doing it to try to make God love us. Even these works are not truly good. No matter what we've done in life, Jesus will remember everything. Good will be rewarded, but bad will be punished, just like another place in the Bible says: we must all appear before the judgment seat of Christ, that each one may receive what is due him for the things done while in the body, whether good or bad (2 Corinthians 5:10).

But the most important thing Jesus knows about us is whether our names are written in the Book of Life. Think of the Book of Life as the list of everyone who is a citizen in heaven, all people who have ever trusted in God for their salvation. When Jesus was on Earth he told his disciples to rejoice because their names are written in heaven (Luke 10:20). This is what He was talking about: all people who have ever trusted Jesus to save them from their sins belong to God.

There are only two places people can go after Judgment Day. If your name is written in the Book of Life, you will join Jesus in new world He will create. If your name is not written in the Book of Life, you will be thrown into a place described as the lake of fire.

Questions for Your Kids:

1. Who is the one sitting on the great, white throne? (*Jesus*)

2. Is this the same Jesus who came and died for the sins of the world? (*Yes. This is the same Jesus.*)

3. Why is it good news that Jesus is the one who will judge us and not someone else? (*Because we know that even though Jesus is our judge, He is not eager to condemn us. He calls to everyone to come to Him, because He is able to and willing to save everyone who comes to Him. Before Judgment Day, He calls everyone to repent and trust in Him.*)

4. Does the idea of going into a lake of fire sound scary to you? (*It should be scary. The Bible also calls this place "hell." What makes hell so terrible is that it is a place of "eternal destruction, away from the presence of the Lord" [2 Thessalonians 1:9]. This will be a place cut off from God and all that God calls good.*)

5. How can we know that our names are written in the Book of Life? (*We can know because Jesus gave us a promise: if we confess that Jesus is the Lord, and if we believe God raised Him from the dead, we will be saved from our sins [Romans 10:9]. If you truly trust in Jesus and if you treat Jesus as your Lord, then you can feel peace believing you really do belong to Him.*)

Prayer: "God, You have fixed a day on which Jesus will judge the world, and You have given us assurance of this by raising Him from the dead (Acts 17:31). We look forward to that day, the day when you even destroy our last enemy death (1 Corinthians 15:26). Judgment Day can be a scary thought, but we know that You will never break Your promises, and You have promised never to condemn those who trust in You. Help us to feel confidence, knowing we are forgiven. Amen."

LESSON 24: Holy Ghost

Opening Thought:

The Apostles' Creed mentions three very important persons: the Father, the Son, and the Holy Ghost or Holy Spirit. Remember that the Father, the Son, and the Holy Spirit are all God. Do you remember when we talked about that? (*See what your child remembers from that lesson. All three persons have been around since before the world was created. All three should be worshipped as God. Perhaps your child remembers the illustration about "Flat Land."*)

The Apostles' Creed says, "I believe in the Holy Ghost" or "Holy Spirit." We talked a little about the Holy Spirit back when we talked about how Jesus was born. Do you remember what the angel Gabriel told to Jesus' mother Mary about how her baby was conceived? (*See what your child remembers from that lesson. Gabriel said the Holy Spirit would do a great miracle and hover over Mary and create in her a human child but without a human father. The child would be the Son of God. The Spirit would also make the child completely holy so Jesus would be born without any sin.*)

There's so much more that can be said about the Holy Spirit, but we'll look at two really important passages.

Scripture Reading: Genesis 1:1-2 and Titus 3:3-7

Explanation: In the first passage, we read that at the beginning of the world, before the world had any shape, God's Spirit was there. We learn here that God's Spirit hovered over the unformed world. This is the same word used of a mother bird hovering over her unhatched eggs, trying to warm them to hatch. This reminds us that God's Spirit is a person, just like God the Father and God the Son. It also tells us that God's Spirit was right there at the creation of the world, bringing life into the world.

In the second passage, we learn that the same Spirit that brought life into the world brings new life to us when we become Christians. In this passage we learn that God pours out the Holy Spirit on us, almost like you pour water out of a bucket. If someone dumps a huge bucket of water on your head, you get completely wet. The water soaks into your clothes and all over your skin. But when God pours His Spirit on us, this doesn't make us soaking wet on the outside, but He does wash us in a more powerful way: He washes us on the inside, in our hearts.

You see, the Bible says without the Holy Spirit, we are all sinners. We are foolish, disobedient, wasting our days away being hurtful to other people, jealous of what other people have or do, and completely ruled by our desires. We don't have the power to do what God wants us to do, and we deserve to be punished by God.

But the good news is God *saves* sinners like us. He does this not because we deserve it, not because we did anything to earn it, but because God is merciful and kind. When we say God "saves" us from our sin, this means a couple different things. First, God forgives us of our sin—He chooses to see us as His children, even though we've acted like His enemies. Second, God also saves us from our sins by renewing us on the inside so that we want to follow God. He does this by pouring His Spirit on us.

You see, a long time ago God made the world, but because we sinned, this world isn't the way it should be. Someday, God is going to make the whole world new again, getting rid of all the sin in the world. Some day the world will be our perfect home again. The Greeks had a word for this: *palingenesia* (pa-len-je-ne-see-uh). It means the *new beginning* or the *new birth* of the world. That's the same word used in this passage.

Think about that: when the Spirit is poured out on us and washes us on the inside, we are really new, but it is only the start of what God will do. Someday, God will change us completely, inside and out, and change our whole world, too. God is going to remake the world, and He is starting with us; He is starting with our hearts.

Questions for Your Kids:

1. So, let's review: Was God's Spirit here at the very beginning when God created the world? (*Yes*)

2. How does the Spirit wash us? What does it mean that His Spirit washes us? (*When we become Christians, He washes us on the inside and cleans the sin out of us.*)

3. When the Holy Spirit washes our sins away, what does this mean? It means at least two really important things. (*First, it means God forgives us of our sins so we are no longer guilty in God's eyes. Second, it means God changes us on the inside, making us new, giving us new desires to love and follow God.*)

4. Has God's Spirit washed you on the inside? (*See how your child reacts to this question. Whether your child says yes or no, ask him or her why. See how much your child understands about the gospel, about Jesus, who He is, why He came, and what He did for us through his death and resurrection.*)

Prayer: "God, thank You for Your Holy Spirit. By faith, You give us the promised Spirit (Galatians 3:14). He is the Spirit of truth that proceeds from You, convicting the world of sin and convincing us about Your Son Jesus (John 15:26; 16:8-10). You give us Your Spirit in our hearts as a guarantee of what is to come (Ephesians 1:13; 2 Corinthians 1:22), so we look forward to the day you make the whole world new. Amen."

LESSON 25: Holy Catholic Church

Opening Thought:

When you think of a church, what do you think about? (*See what your child says. He or she might think of a specific building or a sanctuary. Have your child describe what a church looks like.*)

In the Bible, when you see the word "church," it isn't talking about a special building. It is actually talking about a special group of people. A church is a group of Christians who are coming together so they can worship God. The church is also the group of all Christians everywhere throughout the earth.

The Apostles' Creed says we believe in "the holy catholic church." We're going to talk about what that means as we read this story from the book of Acts.

Scripture Reading: Acts 2:1-8 and 38-42

Explanation: This story takes place seven weeks after Jesus rose from the grave. Jesus told His disciples that after He went to heaven, He would pour out the Holy Spirit on them. Do you remember what we learned about Jesus ascending to heaven? (*See what your child remembers. Jesus stood on the Mount of Olives and started rising into the sky. A cloud of God's glory took Jesus away.*)

Just a few days after Jesus went to heaven, thousands of people were gathered in the city of Jerusalem for a special holy day called Pentecost. They were from all over the empire. It was then that Jesus sent the Holy Spirit down to His disciples. They heard the sound of a strong wind fill the room. Suddenly the disciples saw thin flames of fire appearing over their heads, and suddenly, they were all filled with power. They all began speaking in languages they had never learned before: Aramaic, Hebrew, Latin, Parthian, Iranian, Arabic, and Egyptian—all kinds of languages. Wouldn't that be amazing if suddenly you started speaking a language you never learned before?

Thousands of people were amazed when they heard the sound of the wind and then heard all these people praising God in different languages. Then they heard Peter tell them about how Jesus can save them from their sins. Three thousand people became believers in Jesus that day. Can you imagine how exciting that was?

Why did God give the disciples the power to speak in all those languages? It was because God wanted His people to know that the church was for the whole world: it was for every language of people, every type of person, not just a few. That's what the word "catholic" in the Apostles' Creed means. It means the church throughout the world has all kinds of people; it is meant to be in every nation, every community, every tribe, and it is meant to be in every culture; rich and poor, slaves and freemen, men and women, children and adults. The church is universal.

We don't just believe that the worldwide church is catholic; the Apostles' Creed also says the church is "holy." This means we are set apart for God, we belong to God, and we should live differently than the rest of the world. Even though people from every culture should come into the church, the people in the church should be different than the surrounding world: we should all try to live like Jesus, doing what is pleasing to God, and trusting in God for everything. This is what it means to be holy: God has set us apart for Himself and now we should live like it.

Questions for Your Kids:

1. So, let's review this: what does the word "church" mean in the Bible? (*It means the group of people that God has called out of the world to worship Him.*)

2. What does the word "catholic" mean when it comes to the church? (*It means the church is universal. It is meant to spread throughout the whole world and include every kind of person everywhere.*)

3. What does it mean that the church is "holy"? (*It means that the church is set apart for God, and we should live lives that please God because of it.*)

4. What are ways our family could be more involved with our church? (*Talk to your child about being more involved in your local congregation. See what ideas your child has.*)

Prayer: "God, thank You for the one holy, universal church. Even though the church is spread throughout the world, there is one Lord and one faith that unite us all (Ephesians 4:4-6). Someday every language, every tribe, and every nation will stand before your throne and worship you (Revelation 5:9). Because of Jesus, now all nations of the world can be blessed (Galatians 3:8). God, you are holy, and since You've called us into Your church, help us to be holy, set apart for You, and dedicated to You (1 Peter 1:15-16). Amen."

LESSON 26:
Communion of Saints

Opening Thought:

What do you think is the most important part of your body? (*See what your child says. No matter what part he or she says, ask why. Get your child talking about what makes that body part so important.*)

What part of your body isn't very interesting? (*Get your child talking about this.*)

What if your whole body was just one big [*your child's most important body part*]? What would that be like? (*Help your child see how limited their body would be if they were only one part. What things couldn't your child do?*)

Every part of our body plays a roll in our lives. Every part does something that is helpful. When all the parts work together, your body works the way it is supposed to work.

Today we're going to talk more about the church, the family of God's people. In this Bible passage we're going to read about how the church is like a human body. Listen as I read this.

Scripture Reading: 1 Corinthians 12:12-27

Explanation: When the Holy Spirit is poured out on us, we are united to Christ in a special way. Together we are called "the body of Christ." We are carrying out Christ's important work here on the earth, and just as we are linked to Christ through the Holy Spirit, so we are also linked to each other.

This passage talks about the church like a human body. Some parts of the body might seem more important: our heads so we can think, our eyes so we can see, our ears so we can hear, our mouths so we can speak. The same is true in the church. There might be some people in the church that others look at and think, "They have an important job. They teach people. They lead people. They are more important than I am."

But this isn't true. Every part in the body as a role to play, and every person in the church has an important job. Every person in the church has the Spirit of God in them and they all have special talents and gifts. Some are really good at leading. Others are really good at serving. Some are great speakers and teachers. Others are great at helping someone who is in pain or in need. Some help to organize. Some are great craftsmen and builders. We all have something unique to give.

This passage also talks about making sure we don't feel more important than other people. Maybe we are really good teachers and others admire us all the time: this passage says, "Remember, you need every person in the body just like they need you. You are no more important than they are."

The Apostle's Creed says we believe in "the communion of saints." That's what this passage is about. All Christians are "saints," which means we are all holy people of God. Because we have all had God's Spirit poured out on us, we are all set apart by God as His special people. We are saints.

We are a "communion" of saints. The word "communion" means togetherness, working together, partnering together, being a community, and sharing our joys and sorrows with each other. We all have the Spirit living in us, and its like we're all one body. This is why we should show great love to people in the church, and this is why we should use our gifts and talents to help people in the church. God has brought us all together.

Questions for Your Kids:

1. What does it mean that we are the "body of Christ"? (*It means we are all connected to Christ and connected to each other. God has brought us together into a family, and we work together like a body has parts that work together.*)

2. Who are the people in our church that you think have really important jobs? (*See if your child can think of anyone who is a leader in your church.*)

3. Do you know that you and I also have a special role to play in our church? What are things we could do to serve or help our friends at church? (*See if your child can think of ways to serve people at church. Remind your child that God gives gifts and talents to everyone in the church, not just the people who are leaders.*)

4. If we are all in the body of Christ, how should we care for the other members? (*We should love and support them however we can. When they hurt, we should hurt with them. When they are joyful, we should rejoice with them.*)

Prayer: "God, You are faithful, and You have called us into communion with Your Son, Jesus Christ (1 Corinthians 1:9). Help us to share our resources with those in the church, so we can truly share in the fellowship of the saints (2 Corinthians 8:4). Help us not look to just our own interests, but also the interests of others (Philippians 2:4). You have made those in our church no longer strangers but fellow citizens and members of Your household (Ephesians 2:19). Help us to live like it. Amen."

LESSON 27: Forgiveness of Sins

Opening Thought:

We talked a few lessons ago about Christ coming to judge the world some day. Do you remember anything about that? We read a passage about a great white throne. What do you remember about it? (*See how much your child can recall. Remind them how Jesus will sit on the throne and the earth and sky will flee away. Everyone who has ever lived will be judged. If our names are not written in the Book of Life, we will be cast into the lake of fire, away from the presence of the Lord.*)

We have all sinned against God, and all of us deserve to be judged, but the good news is that God is willing to forgive. That's exactly why He sent Jesus to die for our sins: all who come to Him, He will forgive. In fact, the Apostles' Creed says we believe in "the forgiveness of sins," and this should comfort us.

Forgiveness is what this story from the Bible is all about. This is one of Jesus' most famous stories.

Scripture Reading: Luke 15:11-32

Explanation: Can you imagine the look on the father's face when the younger son told him he wanted his share of his father's money? Back then, you didn't get your parent's wealth until your father was dead, so when the younger son said that, he was saying, "You don't mean anything to me. It doesn't matter to me if you were dead." But his father gave him the money anyway and let him go.

The younger son took that money and wasted it all, and then when the money ran out, he was starving. He took one of the dirtiest, most shameful jobs of all: feeding pigs. His life was very bad. He didn't know what he would do. But finally, one day, he came to his senses. He would go home and beg his father to just be a servant in his house. He knew he had done a bad thing to his father. He didn't just waste his father's money; he also dishonored his father before everyone.

One of the best parts of the whole story is when the father looked down the road and saw the son coming home. He didn't act angry. He didn't scold his son. He didn't even wait for his son to show how sorry he was. He ran down the road, grabbed his son, and hugged him so close and so tight that he buried his face in his son's neck, kissing him. He wouldn't even let his son finish his planned apology. Immediately, the father called for a huge party to be planned. He welcomed his son home, not as a servant, but as a son.

Not everyone thought the father was doing a good thing. Didn't the younger son waste his father's money? Didn't his actions say to his dad, "It doesn't matter to me if you are alive or dead"? Why would the dad be so forgiving? The older son didn't like it at all. The older son just said, "But I'm your good son. I do whatever you ask. Why do you throw a party for this terrible son of yours?" But that's not the way the father thought about it. The father said, "It is right to celebrate, because my son was lost to us, but now he is found!"

That's the way our heavenly Father is when He forgives. He is willing to forgive the worst of sinners, even people who have hated Him and wasted their lives doing terrible things. When we return to Him, He doesn't act mad or mean to us. Jesus actually says, that when just one sinner repents, there is a great celebration in heaven: God is filled with joy when it happens, and He doesn't care if anyone else disagrees with Him.

His forgiveness is complete and total. When we stand before God on Judgment Day, if we have repented of our sin and if we have believed in Jesus, we will not be condemned but we will enter into God's joy.

Questions for Your Kids:

1. Is it difficult to forgive someone if they do something terrible to you? What if someone stole something from you or was cruel to you? Would it be easy or hard to forgive them? (*If your child says it would be easy, then give him or her another example of something really bad that someone could do.*)

2. What does this story teach us about God? (*This story teaches us that God is eager to forgive us when we turn to Him.*)

3. In this story, both sons are wrong. The younger son was wrong because he took all his father's money and ran away. How was the older son wrong? (*The older son thought he could earn his father's love by being good, and he thought his father was being unfair and foolish for forgiving his brother.*)

4. Did the older son need to be forgiven, too? (*Yes. Both sons needed forgiveness: the younger son for being rebellious, the older son for thinking he could earn his father's love by being good.*)

Prayer: "God, our sins have separated us from You (Isaiah 59:2), but in Christ You were reconciling the world to Yourself (2 Corinthians 5:19). His blood cleanses us from all sin (1 John 1:7). You forgive our sins and never bring them up again (Jeremiah 31:34). You trample our sins under your feet (Micah 7:19). You are merciful and gracious, slow to anger, abounding in steadfast love, and forgiving of all our sins (Exodus 34:6-7). Thank You for your grace. Amen."

LESSON 28:
Resurrection of the Body

Opening Thought:

We've talked in previous lessons about how Jesus was raised from the dead. Do you remember all the different witnesses who saw Jesus after He rose again? (*See what your child can remember. Many people saw Him: apostles like Peter, James, and Paul; the twelve disciples saw Him; all the apostles saw Him; even 500 people saw Him at one time.*)

Was Jesus' body the same as it was before He died? (*It was the same body, but it was transformed into something greater. Jesus' body can never die again. His body is no longer weak like all of us, but glorious and powerful.*)

In the Apostles' Creed, when we say we believe in "the resurrection of the body," we are not talking about Jesus' resurrection. We're talking about something that will happen to all of us in the future. Let's read about that.

Scripture Reading: 1 Corinthians 15:51-58

Explanation: Normally, everybody reaches the end of their life and they die. Their bodies remain here on Earth, and their souls leave their bodies. But that is not our final home. Something is coming that is even more amazing.

One day the bodies of the dead will rise up out of their graves—billions of people who have died in the past. Their bodies will be transformed, no longer decaying but alive again. Just like Jesus' body, their bodies will never perish. We will be immortal. If we happen to be alive when this happens, then our bodies will also be transformed.

The dead will rise, and those who are saved will live forever with Jesus on the earth. Those who are not saved will live forever in hell.

When the disciples got to see, hear, and touch Jesus after He rose from the dead, they were getting a preview of what everyone will be like in the future. Someday, Jesus will return and those who are living on the earth will see Him with their own eyes. It is then that God will raise the dead and transform us.

This is an amazing thought. Our final home is not away from our bodies in heaven, but our body and soul living on the earth. After this happens, death will be no more. There will be no more sickness, pain, or disease. Our bodies won't have the same problems we have now. This is because all sin will be gone.

Questions for Your Kids:

1. When God created the world, did He create us with bodies or were we just souls? (*Human beings have always been body and soul.*)

2. After Jesus returns, will we have bodies? (*Yes.*)

3. So, is our ultimate hope our souls going to heaven, or is our ultimate hope heaven coming to Earth? (*Our ultimate hope is that one day heaven will come to Earth and make things right again.*)

4. Some religions believe that this world and our bodies don't really matter because we'll all just die and our souls will go somewhere else. Is this true? (*No. It is true that our souls leave our bodies when we die, but one day our bodies will rise again. God created the world good. One day God will recreate the world and our bodies and everything will be good again. God loves the physical world and our bodies, so we should take care of this world and the people in this world.*)

Prayer: "God, we know the created world is full of decay and death because of sin, and creation longs for the day when it will be set free from death. We also long for the day when our bodies will be redeemed (Romans 8:8-23). When Christ appears, we will be like Him, because we shall see Him as He really is (1 John 3:2). He will transform our lowly body to be like His glorious body (Philippians 3:21). Help us to set our hope fully on the grace that will be brought to us at the revelation of Jesus Christ (1 Peter 1:13). Amen."

LESSON 29: Life Everlasting

Opening Thought:

As we've been studying the Apostles' Creed, we've talked a lot about what life will be like when Jesus comes back. We've talked about how He'll come down to Earth, how he'll change this world and raise the dead. We've talked about how He will judge the world and He will declare that God's people are forgiven for all their sins. What do you think the best part of our eternal home will be? (*See what your child is looking forward to the most. Will it be getting to be with his or her friends and family forever? Will it be having a perfect body? Will it be the perfect world? What will it be?*)

The Bible tells us what the best part of our eternal home will be. See if you can spot it when we read this Bible passage.

Scripture Reading: Revelation 21:1-7

Explanation: The Apostles' Creed says we believe in "the life everlasting," which means we believe that in the new heavens and the new Earth, life will never end. But it means more than this. It doesn't just mean that life will go on forever, but it means that life will be full. It's kind of like when people say, "I feel so alive." They aren't saying that they are alive and breathing; they are saying that they feel lively, full of joy and refreshment. When the Bible talks about eternal life, it is talking about a *full* life that goes on forever.

This passage tells us why life in our eternal home feels so full. Our eternal city will be beautiful, but that's only part of the reason life will be full. There will be no more tears and pain, but that's only part of the reason life will be full. There will be no more death, but that is only part of the reason life will be full.

When heaven comes to Earth, there will be many blessings—riches, comfort, beauty, and peace—but the best part of our eternal home is *who* will be there will us. *God* will be there. This has been God's plan from the beginning. In the beginning, when He created the first people, He walked in their garden in the cool of the day (Genesis 3:8) and spoke to them (1:28-29). In the age to come, when sin and death are finally gone, God will again come to live with us.

God is the one who makes the age to come so wonderful. He is the one who brings our eternal home down to Earth. He is the one who makes it so beautiful. He is the one who wipes away all our tears. He is the one who destroys death forever. He is the one who adopts us into His family and makes us His special children forever.

In this passage, Jesus calls Himself the Alpha and the Omega. Alpha is the first letter of the Greek alphabet. Omega is the last letter of the Greek alphabet. It's like when we say the phrase "A to Z": what we mean is *everything from beginning to end*. Jesus existed before the world began and He will exist forever. He is the beginning of all things and He is the end of all things. We can trust that if He created the world that He will be the one to bring the world to its final goal.

Questions for Your Kids:

1. Imagine what it will be like: one day God's people will get to see God face to face. Can you imagine anything more exiting than getting to see the Creator of the universe? (*Get your child's honest reaction to this idea.*)

2. Why do you think our eternal home is called the "New Jerusalem"? (*Because in the Old Testament, the capital city of God's people was called Jerusalem. It was the place where God's temple was. The New Jerusalem will be home to both God and His people.*)

3. When we say that we believe in "the life everlasting," what does that mean? (*It means that we will live forever and never die, but it also means that the life we will have will be full of joy.*)

4. What will be the best thing about our eternal home? (*God will be there and we will enjoy Him forever.*)

Prayer: "God, we look to our final hope that we cannot see yet, because we know our home is eternal, and it cannot even be compared to our life here (2 Corinthians 4:16-18). There, we will join the eternal feast of the richest foods. You will swallow up death forever. You will take away all our shame. On that day, we will remember that we have waited eagerly for You to come, and we will rejoice in our salvation (Isaiah 25:6-9). The whole point of eternal life is to know You, God, and to know Your Son Jesus Christ (John 17:3). Give us joy now as we think about our eternal home. Amen."

LESSON 30: Amen

Opening Thought:

When people pray, often there's a special word they say at the very end of the prayer. What is that word? (*Amen.*)

Do you know what that word means? (*See if your child knows the meaning of "Amen."*)

"Amen" is an old Hebrew word. Remember, Hebrew is the language that most of the Old Testament was written in, and it is the language God's people spoke. "Amen" means "truly" or "so be it." If someone said something, and you agreed, you might say, "Amen," which means, "Yes, this is true," or "Yes, that will happen." At the end of a prayer, when we say "Amen," it means, "I believe this! I trust in You, God."

Isn't it interesting that we say "Amen" at the end of the Apostles' Creed? Let's learn more about why we do.

Scripture Reading: 2 Corinthians 1:19-21

Explanation: God has made many, many promises in the Bible—so many, it would be hard to count them all. In this passage, the apostle Paul is speaking and he says that every promise from God you can find, no matter what it is, Jesus is the answer to all of them. When we hear a promise from God, we can say "Amen," we can say, "Yes, that's true," because we know Jesus is the answer to that promise.

Think of the Apostles' Creed, which is full of promises about God from the Bible. In the Creed, we say we believe that Jesus will come to judge the living and the dead. We can say "Amen" to that because we believe Jesus came and died and rose again. In the Creed, we say we believe in the forgiveness of sin. We can say "Amen" to that because we believe Jesus died for our sins. In the Creed, we say we believe in the resurrection of the body. We can say "Amen" to that because Jesus has risen from the dead and will use His great power to raise us, too. In the Creed, we say we believe in the life everlasting. We can say "Amen" to that because Jesus lives forever and we are united to Him—so we will live forever with Him.

When Jesus was on Earth, He used to say the word "Amen" a lot, but he used it in a very different way. If you go and read the Gospels, the stories of His life, you'll see that he often began a statement by saying, "Amen, I tell you," or "Amen, Amen, I tell you." This means, "Truly, truly, I tell you this." The Gospels record Him saying this more than 70 times. He wanted us to know that everything He said was absolutely true. Every promise He ever made was absolutely right.

This is why we end the Apostles' Creed with "Amen." We say "Amen" because we believe everything in it is absolutely true.

We also say "Amen" at the end because the Apostles' Creed, isn't just something we say out loud to ourselves. The Apostles' Creed is a prayer. It is a way to worship God. When we say the Apostles' Creed, it is something we say to God as a way to worship Him, and then at the end we should say in a strong voice, "Amen!" When we say "Amen" at the end, we are saying to God, "This is true, God; make all these promises come true!"

Questions for Your Kids:

1. So, let's see if you remember: what does the word "Amen" mean? (*It means "truly" or "yes" or "so be it."*)

2. When we say "Amen" at the end of the Apostles' Creed, what are we really saying in our hearts? (*We are saying, "This is true," and we're asking God to make all these promises come true.*)

3. Jesus is the reason we can say "Amen" at the end of the Apostles' Creed. Why is that? (*Because Jesus is the answer to every promise God ever made. He is the one who guarantees that God's promises are true. He is the one who will make God's promises come true.*)

Prayer: *For your prayer, read aloud the Apostles' Creed in full. You may want to add your own personal prayer at the end.*

I believe in God, the Father Almighty,
the Maker of heaven and Earth,
and in Jesus Christ, His only Son, our Lord:
Who was conceived by the Holy Ghost,
born of the virgin Mary,
suffered under Pontius Pilate, was crucified, dead, and buried;
He descended into hell.
The third day He arose again from the dead;
He ascended into heaven,
and sitteth on the right hand of God the Father Almighty;
from thence he shall come to judge the quick and the dead.
I believe in the Holy Ghost;
the holy catholic church; the communion of saints;
the forgiveness of sins;
the resurrection of the body;
and the life everlasting.
Amen.

APPENDIX: "HE DESCENDED INTO HELL" COMMENTS ON A DIFFICULT PHRASE

"He descended into hell" is perhaps the most controversial phrase uttered in the Apostles' Creed. In some Christian traditions, the phrase has been retranslated, "he descended to the dead," and other traditions have removed the phrase altogether.

The phrase is a late addition to the Creed. There are several minor variations between the Old Roman Creed of the early third century and the received text of the Apostles' Creed of the eighth century, but the phrase *descendit ad inferna*, "he descended into hell," is perhaps the most substantial change.

Is the phrase worth retaining? What does it actually mean?

Meaning of "Hell"

J.I. Packer notes that word "hell," as it is used today, is misleading, because this word has changed meaning since the English translation of the Creed was fixed. Originally, "hell" simply meant the place of departed souls, but since the seventeenth century, "hell" has come to refer to the place of final retribution and punishment. This was not the intent of the English translation.

"Hell" is a translation of the Latin *inferna*. Other ancient creeds that include the doctrine of Christ's descent used *inferos* (Athanasian Creed) or *infernum* (Creed of Venantius Fortunatus). These terms refer to the underworld generally. *Inferos* is where we get our word "inferior"—meaning "under" or "lower."

A loosely corresponding Greek term is *hades*. In the Homeric period, *hades* was perceived as a dull, inactive place of departed spirits, but in the time between Old and New Testaments, both Hellenistic and Hebrew culture developed a richer picture of *hades* as a place of human activity beyond death. *Hades* was no longer a common depot for all departed souls but was divided into compartments for the godly and the wicked, sometimes referred to as "paradise" and "the accursed valley," and separated by a great river or chasm. The accursed valley was often linked to *ge hinnom* (Hebrew) or *gehenna* (Greek), the Valley of Hinnom outside Jerusalem—a deplorable place where refuse from the city was burned that was often used as an image of fiery punishment.

The rabbis, of course, differed on these concepts: some conceived *gehenna* and *hades* as separate locations; others believed paradise was in the heavens, not a separate compartment of the underworld.

In the New Testament, *gehenna* is described as the place of fiery torment, a place where both the body and the soul will be punished after the last judgment, whereas *hades* is described in various ways.

In summary, the Greek *hades*, the Latin *inferna*, and older English *hell* do not refer to the place of final punishment but simply to the world of the dead.

Hell Enters the Apostles' Creed

Writing from northern Italy, Rufinus of Aquileia (AD 354-410) produced his *Commentary on the Apostles' Creed*. In it he pointed out the minor differences between the Creed as he knew it and the Creed as it was used in other parts of the world. He noted that the phrase "He descended into hell" was not used in the church of Rome or the Eastern churches but it was used in his church in Aquileia.

Citing several Scriptures, Rufinus describes Christ's descending to the realm of the dead preaching to the spirits in prison. Christ descended because He was man—and as all men do, He had to experience death in its fullness—but because of the power of His divine majesty, "He was free among the dead, because He could not be detained by death." Rufinus comments that upon His resurrection, "He returned, therefore, a victor from the dead, leading with Him the spoils of hell. For He led forth those who were held in captivity by death."

Rufinus comments further that the phrase's meaning "appears to be precisely the same as that contained in the affirmation *buried*" (emphasis in the original). In other words, while other version of the Apostles' Creed did not contain the descent, they did mention Christ's burial, which (in Rufinus' opinion) implies a spiritual descent.

Rufinus' point is important because some church creeds mentioned Jesus' burial, others mentioned his descent, but the earliest creeds don't mention both together. The Nicene Creed (AD 325) omits the descent and includes the burial. The Athanasian Creed (AD 430) and the creed of Venantius Fortunatus (AD 570) omit the burial and include the descent. Many church historians believe Rufinus is correct: Christ's burial and descent were closely related doctrines—flip sides of the same coin.

What the Early Church Believed

While Rufinus was the first to mention Christ's descent as part of the Apostles' Creed, the concept was not new to creeds in general or to Christian doctrine. Christ's descent is mentioned in the Fourth Formula of Sirmium (AD 359) and creeds published at the Homoean synods (AD 359-360). It is also found in the doxology of the Syria Didascalia and the creed of Aphraates of Persia. In the last century Dom Germain Morin uncovered sermons by Jerome (AD 347-420) where the phrase is included in his creeds as well.

Aside from formal creedal statements, the concept itself dates back much further. The descent was mentioned by Polycarp, Ignatius, Irenaeus, Origen, Tertullian, and many others.

In his book *Early Christian Creeds*, J.N.D. Kelly points out that a full study of these texts shows two broad understandings of Christ's descent. The first interpretation is that while in hell, Christ was preaching salvation, or else administering baptism, to the righteous dead of the Old Testament. For some, this interpretation meant preaching in order to give them a second chance at salvation. For others, this meant proclaiming to them details of the salvation they already possessed in Him.

This interpretation was held by Justin Martyr, Irenaeus, Hippolytus, and Origen. Irenaeus, for instance, comments that he heard from "a certain presbyter who had heard it from those who had seen the apostles" that "the Lord descended to the regions beneath the earth, preaching His advent there also, and the remission of sins received by those who believe in Him." All the patriarchs and righteous men who had prophesied Christ's coming and lived according to God's law heard the preaching of Christ and finally knew how their former sins were forgiven (Against Heresies 4:27).

The second interpretation is that Christ performed a triumphant act of liberation on their behalf, such as Rufinus describes. They believed Christ delivered the saints from Satan, "rescued from the jaws of the cruel dragon," as St. Caesarius put it. In the later centuries of the church, the second line of interpretation became the popular one.

The Overlap of the Bible and Church Tradition

When trying to understand the doctrine of Christ's descent in the Apostles' Creed, there are two overarching concerns. (1) Does the Bible teach it and if so, what does the Bible teach about it? (2) What did the early church mean by its inclusion in the Creed? If the answers to these questions overlap, we will find our answer.

Both concerns are important for interpreting this phrase in the Creed. Some, in an effort to be faithful to the church fathers, embrace the whole of what they had to say about Christ's descent without criticism, ignoring their misinterpretations of the Bible. If we are going to believe the doctrine, the Bible should be our source of revelation about it. Some, in an effort to be faithful to the Scriptures, try to make the phrase in the Creed mean something the church fathers never intended it to mean. If we are going to confess this line of the Creed, we should do so in harmony with the theologians who helped to compose it.

Often Cited Scripture Texts

The church fathers cited many different texts they believed spoke explicitly of Christ's descent. Reviewing major texts, one by one, we can begin to understand the source of the controversy around this doctrine.

Matthew 12:39-40

Jesus says here He will spend three days "in the heart of the earth." Most commentators understand Jesus to be speaking of the grave.

Other commentators, including church fathers like Irenaeus and Tertullian, read it differently. Christ predicts that His experience will parallel that of Jonah, echoing elements found in Jonah's prayer from the belly of the great fish. Jonah says he cried out from the "belly of Sheol" (Jonah 2:2)—translated *hades* in the Greek translation of the Old Testament. Jonah says he was cast into the "heart" of the seas (2:3)—the deepest abyss—just as Jesus would be in the "heart" of the earth. This phrase indicates the lowest depths, not merely a rocky grave on the surface of the earth.

Romans 10:6-7

Paul here contrasts the most inaccessible heights (heaven) and the deepest depths (the abyss). He adopts Deuteronomy 30:12-14, replacing the word "sea" with "abyss," which in the Greek Old Testament usually refers to a great depth of water (Genesis 1:2; 7:11; 8:2; Deuteronomy 8:7), and in one instance (Psalm 71:20) it refers to the realm of *sheol*.

Some believe Paul is speaking hyperbolically. Paul is saying that in order to be saved, we don't have to perform the monumental tasks of ascending into the highest heavens or descending into the lowest depths. Christ has already come from heaven in the incarnation, and He has already come up from the dead—He has brought salvation near already.

Other believe this is a clear indication that the early church believed that just as Christ was once in heaven and came to Earth, Christ's soul also went into the deep abyss of the earth and came up from the dead. This is more than simply a reference to a shallow tomb or the state of death generally, but the underworld itself.

Acts 2:25-32

Peter is quoting Psalm 16 on the day of Pentecost before a crowd of Jews from all over the Empire. This phrase, "you will not abandon my soul to Hades," has been taken a couple different ways.

Some believe it simply means that Christ's soul went to *hades*, but He had confidence that it would not remain there, whereas others believe it means Christ's soul was never resigned to the grip of *hades* in the first place.

Others believe *hades* here simply means "grave" (as some translations have it) or is merely a general term for the state of death. Because Peter's point is that Christ body was raised up, unlike David whose tomb was still occupied in Jerusalem, the text is pointing to Christ being under the power of death or his body being in the tomb, not to the underworld. Under this interpretation, the "soul" of Christ here is not His immaterial person but is instead being used as a personal pronoun (as the Hebrew *nefesh*, or soul, often is).

Ephesians 4:9-10

Paul here is citing Psalm 68:18 and explaining the words in the new context of Christ's victory.

Paul's expression "lower parts of the earth" could mean the earth's lowest regions. Others believe it should be rendered "lower parts, that is, the earth," similar to how we might use the word *of* in the phrase "the city *of* Chicago."

The matter is one of sharp dispute among commentators. Some point out that the word "parts" (*merē*) lacks force if the earth generally is meant, so it must mean the earth's lowest parts. Others respond, saying that it is a single descent that is viewed here, not a two-part descent—first from heaven to Earth and then from Earth to *hades*. Paul's point, they say, is that Jesus humbled Himself in the incarnation.

Luke 23:42-46

This is the story of Christ's conversation with the repentant criminal on the cross. In Jesus' promise to the criminal, He states they will both be in paradise that very day. The Greek Old Testament uses the term "paradise" to refer to both the Garden of Eden (Ezekiel 28:13; 31:8) and the Messianic Age (Ezekiel 36:35; Isaiah 51:3).

Other Jewish literature refers to paradise as the place the elect go when they die, the same place where Enoch was taken (Enoch 60:8). Paul says paradise is in the third heaven (2 Corinthians 12:4), and in the book of Revelation, Jesus said paradise is in the New Jerusalem that comes from heaven to Earth (Revelation 2:7; 22:2). Many believe, based on these references, that paradise must be in heaven, not near or in the underworld.

Still, others believe paradise is not in heaven, but is a compartment of *hades* or that both *hades* and paradise are compartments of the underworld. Many point to Jesus' parable of Lazarus and the rich man (Luke 16) to demonstrate that Jesus' own views echoed that of his Jewish contemporaries who believed that "Abraham's bosom" was a place where the righteous go and await final judgment and resurrection. This phrase, "Abraham's bosom," was a popular way of describing the blessed world of the righteous, as opposed to the *hades* of the damned.

1 Peter 3:18-20

This is perhaps the most cited text for referring to Christ's descent. In this text, we read that Christ's spirit preached to the spirits in prison. Who are these "spirits" to whom Christ made a proclamation? Why did Christ preach to them? To what is this referring?

Many of the early church fathers believed this is a clear reference to Christ's descent into the underworld and His preaching there. Though he was "put to death in the flesh" (His body was dead), he was "made alive in the spirit" (His soul lived on), and as a human spirit he preached to the spirits in prison.

However, others believe the phrase, "put to death in the flesh but made alive in the spirit," is referring to Christ's earthly existence vs. His heavenly life. "Made alive," they argue, usually refers to the bodily resurrection, so being made alive "in the spirit" refers to being resurrected in the sphere and power of God's Spirit. After His resurrection, Jesus went and proclaimed to the spirits in prison, probably at his ascension or enthronement in the heavenly realms.

Others, like Augustine and much of the church since him, do not believe this is referring to something Christ did after His death at all, but something the Spirit of God did long ago. These commentators believe the "spirit" by which Christ was made alive is the Holy Spirit who preached through Noah and others in the days before the Great Flood. Those who heard Noah's preaching and still disobeyed are now the "spirits in prison."

In addition to the question of when this took place is the question of what spirits were the audience. Some believe this must be a reference to human spirits, while others believe the spirits are fallen angels. Only in Hebrews 12:23 are dead human beings referred to as "spirits," and there the context qualifies this. In many other places in the New Testament, spirits are references to angels. Peter could to be referring to fallen angels that disobeyed God in the days of Noah (Genesis 6:1-2). Both Jewish and Christian tradition teaches that these angels were imprisoned for their sins (2 Peter 2:4,9).

Hebrews 11:39-12:2, 12:22-24

While this passage speaks nothing of a descent into hell, it does comment on the state of the saints who departed before the coming of Christ. Hebrews 11 tells of episodes from the lives of famous patriarchs, kings, and saints of old, and then says after their lives were over they were not yet "made perfect." Later, as the author is describing the heavenly Jerusalem that now exists, he says there live the "spirits of the righteous made perfect." How were these saints not yet made perfect before Christ but now are they made perfect? The answer is found in Hebrews 12:2, that they still awaited Jesus, who is the "perfector" of our faith.

Some commentators believe this is evidence that a change took place for the saints in the underworld at the coming of Christ. Some believe this is evidence of the medieval doctrine of the "harrowing of hell." Harrowing is an old English word for removing stones from the field before planting. The belief was that Christ stormed the gates of hell and separated the righteous from the unrighteous, bringing them to a place of blessedness and safety. Others believe the saints were already in "Abraham's bosom" awaiting the coming of Christ, but that by His presence Christ made that place into Paradise.

Possible Interpretations of the Descent

There are a number of popular interpretations of "he descended into hell."

1. Jesus' human soul descended into hades to endure punishment

Several modern preachers claim this view, such as Frederick K.C. Price, Kenneth Copeland, and Paul E. Billheimer. These men believe the cross was only the beginning of our redemption, but Christ needed to suffer in the fires of hell until the resurrection. His pure human spirit had to descend there in order for our redemption to be complete.

This is an unlikely interpretation for a number of reasons. First, it is generally believed that Christ's suffering was finished when He died on the cross. It was before His final breath that he uttered, "It is finished" (John 19:30), and then committed His spirit to His Father (Luke 23:46). Nothing is mentioned in the Bible about additional suffering. Second, this interpretation drastically misinterprets the meaning behind the doctrine as the church fathers understood it. When they spoke of Christ's descent into the underworld at all, it was as a victor, not as a victim.

2. Jesus' human soul descended into hades and offered a second chance at salvation.

This was a belief in the early centuries of the church: some church fathers believed the purpose of Christ's descent was to preach salvation to the lost, giving them a second chance to repent. More recently, E.A. Litton in the 19th century and Wolfhart Pannenberg in the 20th century claimed this view.

While this is one of the views of the early church, this view lacks the support of Scripture. Even if we interpret 1 Peter 3 to mean that Christ preached to departed human spirits after His death, it would go against Peter's overall purpose to suggest that this preaching was to offer a second chance at repentance. If Peter is encouraging his readers to always be ready to give an answer to the unbelieving world about our Christian hope (1 Peter 3:15), all urgency is lost if departed souls have a chance to repent after death. Plus, this interpretation runs against other passages in the Bible that suggests the impossibility of repentance after death (Luke 16:19-31; Hebrews 9:27).

3. Jesus endured hell on Earth and specifically on the cross.

Some believe the phrase about Christ's descent refers to Christ's suffering throughout His whole life, but more especially on the cross, where He faced hellish suffering of His Father's abandonment. This is the position of the Heidelberg Catechism, question 44: "*Why is it added: He descended into Hades?* That in my greatest temptation I may be assured that Christ, my Lord, by his inexpressible anguish, pains, and terrors which he suffered in his soul on the cross and before, has redeemed me from the anguish and torment of hell."

This was also the position of John Calvin who, in his Geneva Catechism, wrote in question 66, "It is immediately added, *He descended into hell.* What does this mean? That he not only endured common death, which is the separation of the soul from the body, but also the pains of death, as Peter calls them (Acts 2:24). By this expression I understand the fearful agonies by which his soul was pierced." Calvin says the phrases before this concerning Christ's crucifixion, death, and burial are what happened to Christ in the visible realm, but His descent into hell is a description of His suffering in the invisible realm.

This position was taught before Calvin and the Heidelberg by Durand of St. Pourcain in the fourteenth century and Pico della Mirandola and Nicolas of Cusa in the fifteenth century. It was also the position of Karl Barth in the modern era.

While it is true that Christ endured great spiritual sufferings on the cross, enduring the wrath of His Father—and Calvin does a masterful job describing this truth—this does not mean that this is the intention behind those who penned, "He descended into hell." It is more likely those who penned the Creed were thinking chronologically, that Christ's descent happened after His death and burial, as the whole Creed is written in a chronological fashion.

4. Jesus descended into hell and proclaimed triumph over the devil.

The Lutheran view is that Christ's soul and body descended into hell. Martin Luther preached, "the entire person [of Christ], God and man, after the burial descended into hell, conquered the devil, destroyed the power of hell, and took from the devil all his might."

While this type of view is in line with many early church theologians, its Biblical warrant is based on a particular reading of some of the key texts mentioned above, such as 1 Peter 3 and Ephesians 4.

5. Jesus' human soul descended into hades and blessed the departed saints.

Some believe Christ departed into *hades* to proclaim His victory to the saints in "Abraham's bosom" (sometimes called *Limbus Patrum* by Catholic scholars). This is the position of Roman Catholics, Anglicans, and other evangelicals.

This is similar to the medieval doctrine of the "harrowing of hell." A harrow was an Old English tool that was used to remove stones from a field before planting. The harrowing of hell refers to Christ entering into the dark and gloomy dungeons below and separating the righteous from the unrighteous—a scene that is depicted on many cathedral frescoes, plaques, and paintings.

Others believe he went so far as to transform the experience of the departed saints by transforming their section of *hades* into paradise by His presence.

This type of view is in line with many early church theologians, but it is based on the theory that paradise was identical to the "Abraham's bosom" of Christ's parable, somewhere in the vicinity of *hades*. This view also holds to the idea that Old Testament saints, by in large, did not go to heaven at death, but went to *sheol*, the realm of all the dead.

6. Jesus truly died and was buried, entering his deepest humiliation.

This interpretation speaks nothing of the place of Christ's soul at death, only that the phrase about Christ's descent is a way to communicate that Christ truly died and was under the power of death. Reformers like Ulrich Zwingli and the Westminster Divines took this view. The Westminster Larger Catechism (Question 50) states: "Christ's humiliation after his death consisted in his being buried, and continuing in the state of the dead, and under the power of death till the third day; which has been otherwise expressed in these words, he descended into hell."

Sheol is often used to speak of the power of death or the danger of death. Louis Berkoff writes, "The words *sheol* and *hades* do not always denote a locality in Scripture, but are often used in the abstract sense to designate the state of death, the state of the separation of body and soul...Since both believers and unbelievers at the termination of their life enter into the state of death, it can very well be said figuratively that they are without distinction in *sheol* or *hades*."

This theory is also very much in harmony with what the early church taught—albeit a very minimalist understanding—and is often based on a particular reading of a number of key texts.

7. Jesus did not descend at all, but rather ascended into the presence of God in paradise.

This is the view held by many theologians, perhaps most notably Wayne Grudem. They argue the phrase is based on incorrect ancient theology. Christ's soul did not descend anywhere. His body descended to the grave and he remained under the power of death, but His soul ascended into heaven to be with God. Christ did not perform any actions in *hades*.

This view would like to see the phrase "he descended into hell" removed from the Creed, going back to earlier versions of the Creed.

The Need for Personal Conviction

The purpose of these reflections is to help you, the reader, get closer to a personal conviction about this theological question. Consult the best commentaries you can. Rely on the wisdom of theologians from ages past. Talk to your spiritual leaders. With a Bible in hand, pray over these matters until you are firmly convinced in your own mind how best to understand Christ's descent into hell.

Get more study resources on this topic at intoxicatedonlife.com.